# FAITHFUL
# FAMILIES

## GIVEN WITH LOVE

TO:

Jen & Trish

FROM:

Ronda

DATE:

September 2019

Happy new home!

# FAITHFUL
# FAMILIES

## CREATING SACRED MOMENTS AT HOME

## TRACI SMITH

**chalice press**

Saint Louis, Missouri

An imprint of Christian Board of Publication

Cover design and images: Paul Soupiset, paulsoupiset.com
Interior design: Grady Campbell Incorporated, www.gradycampbell.com

## ChalicePress.com

PRINT: 9780827211223    EPUB: 9780827211230    EPDF: 9780827211247

Printed in the United States of America

To My Children—Clayton Elias, Samuel Antonio, and Marina Lynn:

May you embrace mystery and wonder, always.
This book is for you.  —Love, Mama

# Contents

**Part Two: Ceremonies**

Chapter 3: *Ceremonies for Marking Life's Transitions*

Chapter 4: *Ceremonies for Difficult Times*

## Part Three: Spiritual Practices

### Chapter 5: *The Spiritual Practice of Prayer*

### Chapter 6: *Ancient Spiritual Practices*

### Chapter 7: *Other Spiritual Practices*

# Acknowledgments

Because this work is a culmination of lessons learned from every facet of life from childhood until now, it is impossible to name every person who had a hand in it. Still, special thanks is due...

...To Chalice Press, for having faith in the premise of this book, and to specific members of that amazing team: Gail Stobaugh for her listening ear and eagle eye, Steve Knight for his laser sharp vision, and especially Brad Lyons for his perspective, enthusiasm, humor and unwavering support from day one.

...To Kerry Grady and Grady Campbell Incorporated for beautiful typography and interior design.

...To my colleagues in The Young Women Clergy Project, soul sisters living all around the country and world: for inspiration, support, and hands-on help. Especially Alex Hendrickson, Kelly Boubel Shriver, and Mihee Kim-Kort.

...To Northwood Presbyterian Church in San Antonio, Texas, for embracing me as their pastor and allowing me space to grow personally and professionally.

...To Marie Scheffers, for being an incorrigible optimist and the truest of friends.

...To Maud Lyon, mentor and friend, for offering encouragement and suggestions when this project was still in its infancy, and throughout.

...To Rev. Doug Learned, for sending me on this path years ago.

...To professors Kenda Dean, George Hunsinger, and Wentzel van Huyssteen, at Princeton Theological Seminary, for teaching me well, and training me for ministry.

...*and, most importantly...*

...To my mother, Lynn Smith, who raised me with a sense of awe, imagination, determination, and spirituality—the very values of this book.

...To my father, Don Smith, who brags about me to anyone and everyone who will listen, and who raised me to believe I could do anything I set my mind to.

...To Scott, Mandie, and the little one on the way. May you use some of the ideas in this book!

...To Ruben Dario, Alexandra, Clayton, and Samuel. You are my inspiration.

Deepest gratitude is reserved for my partner in life, Elias Cabarcas, who believed in this project from the very beginning and provided the space, assistance, and brains to make it happen. Te amo más.

# Foreword

"So we know what we *don't* want to teach him about God," I said to my husband, Dan, as I collapsed onto the park bench, rubbing my pregnant belly. "But we haven't decided what we *do* want to teach him."

It was quiet between us for a moment, save for my labored breathing. A mile around our favorite walking track wasn't as easy as it used to be, but then neither was anything else in those days leading up to and following our first baby's birth.

Dan and I were both raised in loving, grace-filled homes, but in a fundamentalist religious culture that required total acquiescence to a strict set of theological beliefs and left little room for mystery. After years of doubt and deconstruction, we'd made peace with the meandering nature of our own faith journeys, but raising our little boy to do the same seemed daunting. We had no models for that, no roadmap. We knew what teachings we wanted to avoid, but were flummoxed about what to present as an alternative.

"Well I guess it's like everything else with parenting," Dan finally said. "We'll just have to figure it out as we go."

Indeed, parenting, like faith, can only be learned in the doing. So in this first year of being Henry's parents, we've been taking it a day at a time, praying for wisdom, and getting help from those ahead of us on the path—good friends and good guides.

Traci Smith is one of those guides. From the moment I met her, I knew Traci was the kind of mom I wanted to be: playful, empathetic, and deliberate about integrating spiritual practices into her family's everyday life. We met at a Christian women's conference in Texas, and throughout the first day of sessions, Traci insisted on wearing a rather loud, colorful pin her young son had crafted for her to remember him while they were apart. He'd have never known if she'd simply left it in her suitcase, but Traci wore that little pin proudly, and I loved how her eyes twinkled when she talked about her kids.

Traci brings that same joy to the book you now hold in your hands. Faithful Families is a thoughtful, practical guide to teaching by doing—to integrating prayer, tradition, Scripture, and ritual into the routines of a normal, busy family. What I love about this book, and about Traci's work, is how it illuminates the sacred in the everyday, how it invites us to turn a lazy Saturday morning breakfast, a long car ride, the death of a pet, or the end of a stressful day into an opportunity to look for God, hiding in plain sight. "We believe in mystery," she encourages us to tell our kids...and ourselves.

After reading *Faithful Families* (and dog-earing nearly every page for Dan), I felt relieved—relieved I didn't have to understand theodicy before praying a simple blessing over my son's bed at night, relieved I didn't have to know all the answers before staring in awe into a starry sky, relieved I didn't have to be free of doubt to be full of gratitude at our family's "gratitude café." For the first time since becoming a mother, I was thinking less about how I didn't want to parent and more about how I did want to parent, particularly as it concerned my child's spiritual formation.

It's as true for children as it is for adults: faith must be practiced. We can teach, certainly, and instruct and inform. But what will be remembered are those tangible, in-the-flesh actions that get God out of our heads and into our hands. What will be remembered is the scent of a bubbling hot casserole for a family in need, the whoosh of a "Pentecost kite" whipping through the air, the feeling of prayer beads pressed against fingers, the dance of flame atop Advent candles.

As a new parent, I'm often overwhelmed at the prospect of raising a kind and happy son. With this book, Traci reminds us we aren't called to be perfect; we're called to be faithful. All we can do is attend to the present moment. All we can do is take it one step at a time.

— Rachel Held Evans

# Preface to the New Edition —

It's been a little over three years since the first version of this book (formerly entitled *Seamless Faith*) was first conceived. As anyone who spends time with young children knows, a lot can change in three years. My boys, Clayton and Samuel, reinvented their mode of ambulation several times. Right before our eyes, my husband and I watched them transform from scooters to crawlers to walkers to runners in those years. We also learned that we're adding a third precious child to our family, right around the time this new version goes to print!

A lot has changed with the concepts and ideas presented in this book in the past three years as well. Since its initial release I've had the opportunity to connect with so many of you: parents, ministers, children and youth program directors, and more. You've shared your ideas and experiences with these practices, and you've made suggestions about what was missing.

The new edition takes the best of everyone's suggestions and makes the book even better. We've added new practices in every chapter, incorporated links to products or resources that will help you implement the ideas with even less preparation, and added resource guides for ministers and grandparents. Since so many of you give this book away for baptisms, baby showers and other special occasions, we've added a dedication page in the front so you can personalize your gift and create a keepsake for the recipient.

For this second edition I'd like to briefly thank a few people who were a part of the team that put it together: Paul Soupiset for brilliant cover design, the launch team of fifty superheroes and ministers who fielded my numerous crowdsourced questions and ideas, Rachel Held Evans for the lovely foreword, the team at Chalice Press and (most importantly) *you* for picking it up and trying the ideas inside.

I hope you enjoy *Faithful Families* as much as I enjoyed creating it. I would love for you to tell me what you think by visiting www.traci-smith.com or posting on social media with the hashtag #FaithfulFamilies. Let me and other readers know what you've found most useful in this book. What has worked for your family and what has been a challenge? Together we can share ideas and support one another.

Traci Smith, 2017

# Introduction

When my oldest son, Clayton, was four months old, he contracted his first cold. The pediatrician said it wasn't cause for alarm, to monitor him closely, and to bring him back if anything got worse. I spent the whole day worried. I trusted our doctor, but I was a fearful new mom, and my precious baby wasn't well. That evening, my anxiety got the best of me, and I began to conjure up all kinds of worst-case scenarios to the common head cold. At bedtime, as I changed him into his snuggly pajamas and rubbed him down with baby oil, I had an instinct that has now become a ritual in our home. I made the sign of the cross on Clayton's head and said, simply, "Lord, protect Clayton, keep him safe, and heal his little body. Amen." It was a simple gesture, but it felt very profound to me. I was calmer, and my peaceful presence had a positive effect on Clayton as well.

Faith is learned as it is woven seamlessly into the fabric of daily life. I don't intend to ever sit down with my children and "teach" them about the importance of asking God for healing, but they will grow up with that belief as a part of their everyday experience.

This book offers practical ways for families to live their faith together through a variety of ceremonies, traditions, and spiritual practices. These ideas can be practiced from any Christian perspective. Though I am a Presbyterian minister, this book was not written from an exclusively Reformed Protestant perspective. Catholic, Evangelical, Quaker, Unitarian, and even families who do not have a home congregation will find useful ideas in this book.

Part I, Traditions, gives ideas and guidelines for fifteen family traditions. These traditions are designed to deepen a family's life together using faith as the foundation. The most important rule to follow when instituting a tradition is consistency. Traditions lose their impact if they are practiced haphazardly. Chapter 1 contains traditions that can happen at any time of year. The chapter 2 traditions coincide with holy days (holidays) throughout the year.

*Part II, Ceremonies,* describes 15 ceremonies for families to practice at home. They are divided into ceremonies that mark important life events or transitions, and ceremonies for difficult times. For purposes of this book, a ceremony differs from a tradition or a spiritual practice in that a ceremony is an isolated event and does not happen with regularity, as a tradition or a spiritual practice does.

*Part III, Spiritual Practices,* contains 20 spiritual practices divided into three sections. Chapter 5 teaches creative ways families can pray together; chapter 6 contains a variety of ancient spiritual practices adapted to family use; and chapter 7 includes a variety of other spiritual practices. These practices help family members grow spiritually as individuals and as a family.

I encourage families to "pick and choose" from this book. Most families will not choose to use all 50 ideas, but will identify the ones that resonate most closely with their family's style, time constraints, and personality. For ease of use, the ideas in *Faithful Families* are written like a script. Families can follow the script very closely or use it as a guide to create their own traditions, ceremonies, and spiritual practices.

Read on for some frequently asked questions about these ideas, or refer back to this list after you've read through the ideas.

# Frequently Asked Questions

*I haven't been to church in a long time, and I don't know very much about the Bible. What should I know before reading this book?*

You should know that I had you in mind when I wrote it, along with church-going families. The vast majority of these activities do not require any advance knowledge or practice. For those that do, a short introduction is given. It is assumed that parents will be learning these activities alongside their children and experiencing them at the same time.

*What if my child/teenager doesn't want to participate in these activities for family faith?*

There is a balance here, between two extremes. One extreme says, "This is completely optional. You don't have to do it if you don't want to." The other extreme says, "You will do this because we said so, and you will like it!"

The first extreme, being too lax, gives an easy out when it comes to faith. After all, when parents believe something is important, they insist on it. If a child says, "I don't want to go to school," even day after day, quitting school still isn't an option. Parents find a way to insist on school attendance, knowing that the skills learned in the classroom will pay dividends in the child's life in adulthood. This is true of faith and spiritual practice as well. Sometimes the practice becomes more meaningful or enjoyable with effort, and, if we don't put in the time and energy, we never reap the reward. The second extreme, rigidly insisting on 100 percent participation all the time, can backfire as well. Constantly badgering children to be involved with activities that don't resonate with them, or which annoy them, will eventually lead them to resent faith and spirituality.

One way to find a healthy balance is to insist that children try something once or twice, or to insist that they are present even if they are not participating. If the children seem to routinely resist the activities, give them a break for a few months and try again. This book has a variety of activities intended to reach a wide range of children. Keep at it, gently, and you will often find something that works well for your family. Note: faith traditions, ceremonies, and spiritual practices should never be used punitively. ("If you don't shape up, you'll have to...") These ideas are designed to encourage openness, creativity, and healthy spirituality in your children, not to bully them into having faith.

*What should I do when something goes wrong?*

This book is based on the premise that sharing spirituality as a family and deepening your faith together is often a journey of discovery. Families will find activities in here that work well for their context and others that don't work as well, or even at all. Each family is unique. Use this book as a guide, and an invitation to experiment. When something goes well, rejoice! When one of the activities falls flat for your family, let it go. Before you do, though, give it a second or even a third chance. Some of the practices in this book become more meaningful with time. Also, make use of the "Variations" portions of the activities to adapt ideas for your family.

*My children are far apart in ages and have wildly different personalities; how will we make these ideas work as a family?*

Each idea has several variations to accommodate differences in children's ages and personalities. In some families, certain family members will be more drawn to a particular variation. There may be some activities that are particularly loathed by a family member or two. Take an experimental approach, and don't force a child to participate in an activity more than a few times if she or he has demonstrated dislike for it. Along the same lines, take care not to negatively compare siblings in these activities. If one child is not enjoying an activity that another loves, use it as an opportunity to point out that God speaks to individual people in different ways.

*How old should my children be to take part in these activities?*

There are activities in this book for children of all ages, from babies to adolescents. The suggested ages are listed at the beginning of each activity. The ages listed in each idea are approximate. They were identified using my experience and knowledge of children's faith and psychological development at various stages. Some children, however, will be ready for an activity far earlier than the age listed, whereas others will need to wait even longer until they are ready. Parents are advised to experiment and use their instincts about what is best for their children.

*What is the theological perspective of this book?*

My own theological leanings are rooted in a reformed Christian perspective, having been aligned at various points in my faith journey with the United Church of Christ (UCC), Christian Reformed Church (CRC), and Presbyterian Church (PCUSA). Also, as a minister and a parent, it's my hope and prayer that my children and the children I pastor will learn to understand the world theologically and spiritually, no matter where they find their faith community as adults. This book provides the framework of spirituality on which the "walls" of any particular tradition can hang. I encourage you to adapt these ideas to your own faith perspective and to seek guidance from your minister, pastor, or priest for ideas about how to incorporate elements from your unique tradition into these activities.

This book, while rooted in Christian faith, does not shy away from using examples and images from other faiths, knowing that the world is a diverse place. Teaching concepts from other faiths alongside one's own helps children to learn tolerance and acceptance for others. It also helps children understand what their faith has in common with other faiths.

*I did one of the activities in the book, and my child asked a question about God I couldn't answer. What should I say or do when that happens?*

Children have so many questions about the world around them, including faith and spirituality. "What happens when we die? How do we know there is a Spirit when we can't see it? If God is good and loving, why do bad things happen?" I encourage parents to embrace a single word when it comes to these tough questions: mystery. To say to children, "We believe in mystery," is a powerful thing. It's important not to use mystery lightly with children. To teach mystery is to embrace the truth that we don't know everything, rather than run from it. When a child asks a question that is answerable only through faith, say, "That is a wonderful mystery of our faith. Many people have different ideas, but most people say we can't know all of these answers while we are on earth. What do you think?" As children grow, they are able to engage spiritual and theological dialogue in even greater depth.

*I am a pastor/youth minister/children's minister. How should I use this book?*

This book is a tool for you. Use it to give ideas to parents in your congregation who come to you saying, "I want my children to grow up with a sense of faith, but I don't know where to start!" There are also several ideas in this book in which clergy participation with a particular family is encouraged. As you read through the ideas, consider how you might adapt them for your congregants' needs and theological leanings.

**A note about gender language**
As children hear their parents or other adults talk about God, they begin to form an opinion of what this God must be like: Is God loving or hateful? Is God near to us, or far away? Is God a man, or a woman? Christians affirm that God is neither male nor female, yet so many children think of God as an old man. One of the ways to help break out of this mold and help your children think of God beyond gender is to take out "he" when referring to God. This book refers to God in gender-neutral ways.

# Get Ready: *Create a Sacred Space*

Many of the traditions, ceremonies, and spiritual practices in this book would be enhanced by having a sacred space in your home. A sacred space can be permanent—a room transformed into a family sanctuary —or it can be temporary—the living room transformed for a time.

Whether the sacred space is temporary or permanent depends on space considerations and family preference, but the following guidelines are useful for creating sacred space no matter the size or permanence of the space:

*Comfort*: Comfort is key in a sacred place! Soft cushions or chairs, blankets, and hammocks are all perfect for a sacred place. If there are older members of your family who don't transition easy to or from the floor, make sure there is a chair available. Allow children to sit or lie on the floor.

*Clutter:* Keep clutter under control in the sacred space. It's difficult to focus on spiritual matters when there is visual clutter in the space.

*Senses:* Engage all of the senses in a sacred space. What does the space look like? How do the blankets and chairs feel? Does it smell nice there? Is the sacred space free of unwanted electronic buzzing or other noise?

*Inclusiveness:* A family sacred space should have special elements for each member of the family. Allow each person to pick one piece of art or other element for the space.

*Simplicity:* Don't crowd the space. Allow it to be a place where the mind can wander and energy can move and flow.

# Part One

---

## Traditions

# Chapter 1

*Traditions for Every Day*

# Bedtime

*Night Time Blessing*

In addition to (or instead of) evening prayers, a bedtime blessing from parents is a wonderful tradition. Not only can it be done with children who are too young to speak, but it frees a busy child from the need to do or say anything. The blessing is simply received. It is a gift from the parent and an expression of the child being loved by God. Consider using the same blessing night after night so your child may begin to internalize and anticipate it.

**Designed for Newborn through School Age**
(As long as children are being tucked into bed by parents)

**Time Investment:** 30 seconds—1 minute

**Materials:** None

**How To**
1. At bedtime, after the child has finished his or her usual bedtime routine (teeth brushed, pajamas on, story read, etc.) say to your child, *"Daddy (or Mommy) is going to say a night time blessing now!"*

2. Place your hand on the child's head or shoulder and say a short blessing. Use one of the examples or write your own.

i. [Child's name], may God bless you and keep you.
May God be kind and gracious to you.
May God give you peace tonight and every night. Amen.[1]

ii. [Child's name], may the peace of God, which is bigger *than anything we understand, fill your heart and your mind, and may you know God's love always. Amen.[2]*

*iii. [Child's name], may the God of hope fill you with joy and peace, not only tonight, but tomorrow and the next day and all the days of your life. Amen.*[3]

*iv. God Bless [child's name]. Amen.*

3. At the end of the blessing, say, *"Amen,"* give the child a hug or kiss, and leave the room.

**Notes**
- The bedtime blessing can be shared by whichever parent or caregiver is putting the child to bed. The consistency in the blessing through a variety of different people provides a sense of security and safety to children.

- There is no age too small for this blessing. Begin to bless your children at bedtime from their very first day of life!

**Variations**
- Write the blessing or type it, and put it in a frame it over the child's bed.

- Allow older children to say a blessing to parents as well.

- Have a time of bedtime prayers and do the blessing at the end.

# Bedtime

*Marking the Days God Has Given*

When my son Clayton was about 18 months old, we began to add a sticker to a piece of poster board every night before bedtime. The original idea was to keep track of books we were reading, but it became more than that. Removing a sticker and affixing it to the poster board had a sort of ritual feel to it. It wasn't a "reward" for reading a book anymore; it was a moment to mark the fact that another day was through and that it was time for bed. This tradition is inspired by that same tradition I started with Clayton. Much like writing in a daily journal or marking off the days on a calendar, this tradition says, simply, "Another day has come and gone." As the days go by, the stars on the board become more numerous, and a simple piece of art is created. It's powerful to look at the board after a few months of this tradition.

**Designed for Ages 18 Months—5 Years**

**Materials**
1. Piece of poster board
2. Small star stickers

**Time Investment:** 30 seconds—1 minute per night

**How To**
1. Every evening, just before bed, walk to the poster board, choose a star sticker and place it on the poster board.

2. Say, *"Thank you, God, for another day. Amen."*

**Notes**

- This tradition is particularly effective for little ones. While they might not understand some of the spirituality behind marking the days God has given, they will still appreciate the tradition and routine feel of it. As they grow, the conversational aspect can grow and develop as well.

- Like some of the other traditions in this book, this tradition is effective in its simplicity. Some of our days are challenging; some are easy. This tradition thanks God for the day and does not offer commentary.

- Another beautiful thing about this tradition is how the days accumulate over time. Each of the stars represents a day, and over time it is impressive to think about the days, and the joys and challenges they presented.

**Variations**

- Use stickers with varied shapes or symbols.

- Put the stickers in a book rather than on a poster board.

- Say a prayer after putting the sticker on the poster board.

- Decorate or paint the board before hanging it.

# Morning

*Gratitude Cafe*

One of my parishioners, a busy professional and mother of two, once told me, "In the morning, I take my coffee out to the porch and take a few minutes to reflect on everything I'm grateful for. This is how I find God and keep sane." This tradition is a version of her tradition, adapted for family use. Gratitude has been proven, time and again, to be a value that increases health of all kinds: spiritual, mental, and physical. To take a moment and reflect on all of life's many blessings, even once a week, is a worthwhile endeavor.

**Designed for Ages 8+**

**Materials**
1. A variety of morning beverages (tea, coffee, orange juice, hot chocolate)
2. Pencils and pens

**Time Investment:** 15—20 minutes

**How To**
1. Choose how often the family will hold the gratitude cafe. Weekly? Monthly? Daily? I suggest weekly, though some families will find this too frequent or infrequent for their needs.

2. On the morning of gratitude cafe, wake up early, make a special beverage for each family member, and gather someplace together. Outside can be a nice option, depending on space and weather conditions.

3. Say, *"There are so many things for which we can be thankful: the air we breathe, the home we live in, the clothes we wear. Let's each*

*take a moment and write down some of the things we are thankful for. Let's try to each write down five things, and then we will share them."*

4. After a time of silent writing, say, *"Let's share the things we are thankful for with one another."*

5. Once everyone has shared, close by saying, *"God, we are thankful for all of these blessings, Amen."*

**Notes**

- Gratitude cafe is listed in the traditions section because it is, ideally, practiced with some degree of regularity. Over time, family members will begin to anticipate the gratitude cafe moments and look forward to reporting specific things for which they are thankful. Try to incorporate it at regular intervals throughout your family's life.

- Saturday mornings are a great time for many families, as are Sunday evenings. If the cafe moment needs to be cancelled for some reason, make an effort to reschedule within a day or two.

- Some may need prompting for this activity, especially at first. Ask leading questions:

*Are you thankful for any material blessings of this past week?*

*Thankful for anything special we have done as a family?*

*Thankful for any lessons you have learned?*

*Morning: Gratitude Cafe*

---

- Parents and adults can model what it means to be thankful in all circumstances by highlighting the lessons they've learned from mistakes, or the hidden blessings in difficult circumstances.

**Variations**
- At the end of the tradition, put the slips of paper in a basket and use them for the New Year's tradition "Remembering God's Blessings in the Past Year." (See chapter 2.)

- Have younger children draw pictures instead of writing.

- Encourage family members to hold individual gratitude cafes each day, and then compare notes at the end of the week.

# Morning

*Prepare for the Day to Come*

As we embark on each new day, sometimes we wearily open our eyes and find that we are in need of energy, or courage. There are other days when we wake up with anxiety or nervousness and find we are in need of peace and calm. On still other days, we are in need of joy or self-control, or something else. For this simple tradition, family members take a moment at breakfast and reflect on what the day might bring. Each person identifies the thing he or she most needs for the day ahead, choosing the appropriate card and putting it in a pocket to use as a prayer and hope for the day.

**Designed for Ages 6+**

**Materials**
1. Empty box
2. Index cards, cut in half
3. Markers
4. Scissors
5. Clear contact paper or laminating machine (optional)

**Time Investment**
30 minute initial investment to make the box, and then 10 minutes daily whenever the tradition is practiced

**How To**
1. Cut index cards in half. Make several cards with each of the following words:

*Love - Grace - Peace - Joy - Kindness - Friendship - Patience - Mercy - Self-Control - Courage - Compassion - Honesty - Calmness - Energy - Friendship.*

*Morning: Prepare for the Day to Come*

---

2. Leave several cards blank, as well.

3. Laminate the cards with either a laminating machine or using clear contact paper (optional).

**For the Tradition**

1. In the morning, sit together as a family and talk about the day ahead. What significant things are happening in the day? What do you need for the day?

2. Pick what you need out of the box and carry it with you for the day in your purse, backpack, or pocket. Return it to the box at the end of the day so that it might be taken again another day.

**Notes**

• Parents might feel tempted to use this exercise as an "information-gathering" session. If a child mentions needing courage because of a difficult situation at school, the instinct might be to say, *"Oh, really, what's the situation? Is someone picking on you? Are you in trouble? Does it have to do with that girl, Martha?"* etc. Try to resist the urge to do this, instead saying, *"Anything else you would like to share about that?"* Encourage family members to share as little or as much as they feel comfortable sharing. The focus of the tradition is to be quiet before God and to reflect on the day ahead.

• If your family practices this tradition daily, it will be necessary, from time to time, to reevaluate the box and replenish it because the cards may get lost in pockets, shoved into bags, etc.

- The blank cards in this exercise are meant to represent a value or quality that is not listed here. When the cards are passed around, tell family members that they can select something that is not in the box.

**Variations**
- Eliminate the sharing time and leave the box by the door. Allow family members to sift through it and take what they need for the day.

- Gather together at the end of the day to evaluate how the day went for each of the family members, and how they experienced the thing they were hoping to receive throughout the day. (See also, "The Ignatian Examen," in chapter 6.)

# Mealtime

---

*Grace Meals*

Taking a meal to an individual or family in need is a tangible expression of love and concern. Many communities of faith practice this tradition by organizing meals for those who are grieving, suffering from chronic illness, or experiencing a life transition. This tradition involves taking the same meal you are eating to a family who needs a meal. The connection between the two families is solidified as you discuss and pray for the other family while you eat your own meal.

**Designed for Ages 4+**

**Materials**
Dinner for your family and another family. It's nice if it is homemade, but this is not a requirement. The meal can be store bought or takeout.

**Time Investment:** Varies

**How To**
1. Decide how often your family will have a grace meal. For some families, having a structured time will work well and ensure that the tradition is maintained. Perhaps a monthly or quarterly grace meal will be a good fit for your family. For families that love to cook and eat together, perhaps you will celebrate a grace meal every other week, or even more often.

2. A couple of days before the grace meal, identify who will be the recipients. Check with your church or other groups for families who have special need of food, if a family doesn't immediately come to mind. Check with the family who will be receiving the meal and confirm the following:

- The date and time for the meal to be delivered

- Any allergies or special preferences of the family receiving the meal.

3. On the day of the grace meal, involve the whole family in the preparation of the meal. Remember to make a double portion of everything—half will go to the family receiving the meal; the other half will be your family's dinner for the evening.

4. Package the dinner for the recipient family and take it to them.

5. Return home to eat your portion of the same meal. Before you begin, give thanks to God for the family who is also eating the grace meal, praying that they will feel God's love and care through the meal.

6. If appropriate, talk about the other family during your meal and ask questions about how your family might continue to serve and bless them.

**Notes**
- Model the true spirit of this activity: hospitality. (For more on this, see "Hospitality," in chapter 7.) Rather than being elaborate or fancy, it is more important that the meal be served with love and care for the recipient family.

- In my experience, this is a good time to use a tried and true family favorite recipe, rather than experimenting with something new. That way, there is less chance it will turn out differently than expected for both families!

*Mealtime: Grace Meals*

- When people are sick, grieving, or in the midst of a life transition, they often don't feel up to hosting guests, To deliver a meal and allow the family to eat it at a time of their own choosing allows them privacy and freedom.

**Variations**
- Have a signature "Grace Meal" that your family always prepares (assuming there is no one in the recipient family who has allergies or aversions to the food you have chosen). It could be something simple that includes a main dish, side dish, and dessert (for example, spaghetti, salad, and brownies; or soup, bread, and cookies).

- Get take-out for both families.

- Color placemats or cards to include with the meal.

- Have "Grace Desserts" that accomplish the same goal, but through dessert.

# Marking the Passage of Time

*Color Your Year*

Department stores tell us what season it is: tinsel and Santa Clause at Christmas (though sometimes beginning as early as September now), teddy bears and roses at Valentine's day, eggs and bunnies at Easter. Store displays are constantly trying to get ahead of the season and push the culture forward. Though I have always been resistant to the commercialization of holidays, I do appreciate being able to mark the passage of time by seeing a change in scenery. This year-round activity helps your family keep track of the seasons in the Christian year (Lent, Easter, Advent, Pentecost, and Ordinary Time). A table in the home is selected to have a tablecloth that changes colors based on the liturgical season. Though the change is subtle, the effect, over time, is noticed.

**Designed for All Ages**

**Materials**
Side or end table dedicated to this purpose and simple tablecloths in the following colors: green, red, white, purple

**Time Investment:** Varies

**How To**
1. Choose an end or side table in your home that will serve to mark the passage of time through colors. The table will usually have a green cloth, representing "Ordinary Time." Green represents life.

2. Change the cloth from green at the following times:

  • Four weeks prior to Christmas: Purple. During Advent purple represents the coming of the King into the world.

*Marking the Passage of Time: Color Your Year*

---

- Christmas Day until Epiphany (January 6): White. White during this time represents the joy of Christ coming into the world.

- Four weeks before Easter (Lent): Purple. Purple during this time represents repentance and solemnity.

- Easter and six Sundays afterward: White. White at Easter and after Easter represents the newness of our life with Christ.

- Pentecost (late May–early June [varies], check calendar): Red. Represents the fire of the Holy Spirit.

**Notes**

- If your congregation follows the liturgical calendar, you will find that the colors on your chosen table will usually match the colors chosen in worship. However, this "home version" of liturgical colors is simplified to make it easy to manage. Because of this, the colors on the table will probably not always match the colors at church. One example of this would be a change to white for Christ the King Sunday and Trinity Sunday.

- Some congregations choose blue instead of purple during the Advent season to distinguish Christmas and Easter. If this is the practice of your congregation, consider using a blue cloth during these weeks.

- Babies and toddlers won't be able to grasp much significance in the color change, but can still learn to notice the change as they are learning about color.

**Notes**

- In time, some of these activities may "rise to the top" and become favorites. Similarly, some might not work well for your family and will disappear from the rotation.

- Find times when your family is particularly prone to stress and anxiety and try to incorporate one of these activities in advance. Some families might like to keep the Sabbath ideas in the car.

- Visit www.traci-smith.com/resources for links to poems or musical pieces referenced in this activity.

**Variations**

- Add additional colors for different time periods (three minutes, ten minutes, twenty minutes, one hour) and come up with your own activities for each that are well suited for your family.

- Instead of grabbing a Sabbath activity at random, pick a particular time of the day or week to do a Sabbath activity.

- Take the cards out of the basket after each Sabbath time until all have been chosen.

# Chapter 2

*Traditions for Holidays (Holy Days)*

# New Year's Eve

*Remembering God's Blessings in the Past Year*

### Designed for School Ages and Older

### Materials
1. Basket/box labeled with the year (2017, 2020, etc.)
2. Pencils and scraps of paper

### Time Investment: Varies

### How To
1. In January, place a large box or basket in a prominent location in the house with the year labeled on it.

2. Throughout the year, put significant items in the basket, such as ticket stubs, programs, church bulletins from important holidays, etc.

3. Also, use scraps of paper to write down or draw pictures of important memories and things that happened.

4. On New Year's Eve, take turns pulling items out of the basket and reflect upon where God was present in that day.

5. Conclude by holding hands and saying, *"Thank you, God, for the many ways you were with us last year, in good times and in difficult ones. We are thankful for the many blessings of this year. Amen."*

### Notes
- It might be tempting to put only happy memories in the box, but consider also adding memories of more challenging times as well

(evidence of hospital stays, bulletins from the death of a loved one, etc.). God is with us in good and difficult times, and it's valuable to remember sad times, too.

- The age listed for this activity is school age and up. Certainly younger children can be a part of the family moment in which the memories are shared and recalled, but it might be more challenging for them to remember to add to the basket.

**Variations**
- Instead of collecting memories throughout the year, try to sit down on New Year's Eve and remember key moments throughout the past year.

- Use the sacred meal (chapter 6) as a time to write down memories.

- Gather together on a specific day of the week to write down memories to add to the box.

# Epiphany

*A Guiding Star for the Year to Come*

Epiphany, on January 6, is the official end of the 12 days of Christmas. Many Christians celebrate this day by remembering the journey of the Magi. The Magi found their way to Jesus by following a bright heavenly body, usually represented by a star. This activity allows each member of the family to pick out a star that will guide him or her throughout the coming year.

**Designed for Ages 10+**

**Materials**

1. 25 paper stars labeled with the star words listed below:

*Grace - Mercy - Love - Faithfulness - Peace - Patience - Kindness - Joy - Rest - Adventure - Attention - Imagination - Faith - Compassion - Friendship - Song - Art - Generosity - Time- Humility - Persistence - Dedication - Inspiration - Comfort - Wholeness*

2. Box or basket large enough to hold the stars

**Time Investment:** 15 minutes, plus 30 minutes to prepare stars

**How To**

1. This tradition is meant to be held on January 6, Epiphany. Ahead of time, one person in the family makes the 25 stars with the words on them and places them face down in the basket. When the family has gathered together, read Matthew 2:10–12 out loud together. It says, *"When the wise men saw the star, they were filled with joy. They came to the house where the child was and saw him with his mother, Mary, and they bowed down and worshiped him. They opened their gifts and gave him treasures of gold, frankincense, and myrrh" (NCV).*

2. Say, *"This story is a story about how the Magi (or wise men) came to Jesus and brought him gifts. They determined which way to go by following a star. Today we are going to pick out our own star to guide us in the year to come. We will each reach into the basket and pull out a star that will be our guide for this year."*

3. [Note: This step is skipped the first year.] Say, *"Before we pick out our star for this year, let's reflect on the star that was our guiding light last year. What was your guiding star last year? What did you think about it? How did you see it as your guiding light during the year?"*

4. Say, *"As we leave, we will each pick out a star to guide us for the coming year. We will pick one out of the basket, and not share what we have received with each other until next year. May we each be guided by our chosen star and find wonderful things this year. Amen!"*

5. Everyone leaves by saying, *"Happy Epiphany!"*

**Notes**

- This activity requires a fairly advanced level of abstract thought. What does it mean to be guided by hope, for example? For this reason, the age is listed as 10+. For younger children, try one of the variations below.

- Teens in particular may feel a special connection to this activity because of its "secret" component. If you have teens in your home, give this one a try!

- In contrast to most of the activities in this book that are created together as a family, I advise that one person be in charge of making

*Epiphany: A Guiding Star for the Year to Come*

---

the stars in advance of this activity. This allows the words to be a surprise to those who pick them out. As the stars become less numerous through the years, new ones can be added.

- This idea is based on a practice I found in the September 2009 issue of *Reformed Worship Magazine.* See: http://www.reformedworship. org/article/september-2009/star-gifts

**Variations**
- Make and decorate stars and hang them up in your house to remember and commemorate this day.

- With younger children, instead of having individual stars, choose just one star as a family and let that star guide the whole family for the year to come.

- Take turns preparing the stars and coming up with words that will be used year after year.

# Three Pillars of Lent

*Prayer*

The first pillar of Lent is prayer. Though there is an entire chapter of *Faithful Families* devoted to prayer (chapter 5), prayer is also included here as a Lenten practice. This practice invites families to devote 40 complete days to prayer by focusing on a different word each day (excluding Sundays).

**Designed for Ages 6+**

**Materials**
Varied

**Time Investment:** 10 minutes or less per day

**How To**
1. At the beginning of Lent, make a list of 40 words that your family will use to anchor your prayer practice. Use the 40 words listed in the "notes" section, or think of your own.

2. At the start of each day (except Sundays during Lent), take a look at the day's word. Make sure everyone knows what the word is and commits to trying to think about the word throughout the day.

3. At the end of the day, gather for prayer time as a family. Review the word and discuss it in one of the following ways:

• Draw a picture that represents the word.

• Share a photo you took of something that represents the word.

• Share what the word means to you, or how it affected you throughout the day.

*Three Pillars of Lent: Prayer*

---

- Share how the word might be connected to the Lenten journey.

4. Close by thanking God for the word and looking forward to the next day's challenge.

**Notes**

- If you don't want to come up with your own words, here are 40 you can use.

| | |
|---|---|
| 1. Hope | 21. Despair |
| 2. Strength | 22. Weakness |
| 3. Light | 23. Fire |
| 4. Fear | 24. Walk |
| 5. Love | 25. Crawl |
| 6. Freedom | 26. Run |
| 7. Peace | 27. Purple |
| 8. Quiet | 28. Cross |
| 9. Dark | 29. Grace |
| 10. Cold | 30. Gift |
| 11. Water | 31. Reflection |
| 12. Peace | 32. Remember |
| 13. Witness | 33. Eat |
| 14. Noise | 34. Shadow |
| 15. Desert | 35. Want |
| 16. Kindness | 36. Mercy |
| 17. Friends | 37. Justice |
| 18. Strangers | 38. Lonely |
| 19. Heaven | 39. Silence |
| 20. Wait | 40. Resurrection |

- The Spirit works in mysterious ways through prayer. It's fine if the photos, drawings, and stories that come out as a result of the prayer conversation don't feel "spiritual" or don't appear to have anything to do with Lent. Sometimes prayers that seem to lack significance at the time come to have meaning days, weeks, or even years later.

- If you miss a day, just pick up again where you left off.

**Variations**
- Instead of gathering as a family to discuss each word, gather once each week or once at the end of Lent to discuss how this went. This option might be particularly appealing for teens or older children who are interested in journaling and might not wish to share each day's photo, drawing, or thoughts.

- As with the other two Lenten practices, these work well in larger groups. See if other families will join you for this Lenten practice.

- Decide on the words together as a family before beginning.

# Three Pillars of Lent

*Fasting*

Fasting, the second pillar of Lent, is possibly the most implemented practice of a Lenten discipline, particularly for folks who come from a Roman Catholic background. For some, fasting includes abstaining completely from food during the day, or on certain days. For others, fasting means giving up chocolate or treats (or some other luxury) for the entire forty days of Lent. I encourage families to try mini-variations of some of these fasts during Lent, and especially encourage a fast from screens and technology. The purpose of a fast is not to give something up just for the sake of austerity or challenge (although we can all be challenged as we practice spiritual discipline), but rather so we can focus more on God in the absence of that which we are giving up.

**Designed for Ages 8+**

**Materials**
None

**Time Investment:** Varies (see "How To")

**How To**
1. Decide together, as a family, how long the screen fast will last, and for how long. The "buy-in" from the whole family is the most important and most challenging part of implementing this practice. Consider these questions for discussion as you decide:

- *Why do we want to do a technology fast as a family? How will it help us, spiritually?*

- *Should we try a fast for a short period of time every day or for a long period of time once per week? (technology fast for 30 minutes per day vs. all day every Sunday)*

- *Which activities would be excluded from the fast?* An example might be answering phone calls on a smartphone in case there is an emergency (while not using it to text, check social media, etc.).

- *What will we do if someone breaks the fast? How should we gently remind each other?*

- *What will we do when the fast is over? How will we celebrate?*

2. At the start of the technology fast, gather together and have a short conversation about the fast, reminding everyone of the mutually agreed upon parameters from step one. Start the fast with a short prayer: *"God, thank you for guiding our family as we made this decision to focus on you and one another by laying our technology aside for awhile. Please help us on this journey to encourage one another and learn new things. We ask for your Spirit's help in this, Amen."*

3. End the fast with some sort of celebration together, such as a family outing or meal.

**Notes**
- This is a spiritual exercise, designed to help reinforce the idea that giving up or letting go of something, while difficult, can lead to spiritual growth and development. This is a very different framework than house rules, though the two overlap. In other words, a parent might choose to institute a "no screens during dinner" rule or a "no screens between the hours of 8 p.m. and 8 a.m." rule, knowing

*Three Pillars of Lent: Fasting*

---

that it's healthy and good to detach from technology. I would agree wholeheartedly with rules like this, but I advise that parents understand that there's a difference between a rule and a spiritual practice. Spiritual practices should be undertaken voluntarily. If a voluntary technology or screen fast is too much of a sticking point for your family, try one of the variations below.

- After agreeing all together to the parameters for the fast, answering the question, *"What will we do instead?"* is the most important key to the success of this fast. If there's not a clear idea of what will be done *instead* of the screen time, frustration and resentment may grow.

- As with any spiritual practice, start slow and short and increase the time with practice, especially if your family is not used to screen-free time. There's no shame in beginning where you are. If 15 minutes per day is all your family can agree to, so be it. Perhaps try 20 minutes the next week, and so on.

**Variations**
- Agree to a fast from something else as a family. And, instead of only giving something up, think of a way to turn it into a positive. A few ideas:
  — Fast from sweets and desserts and donate the money saved to a food pantry.
  — Fast from dinners out and invite friends over for dinner instead.

- Try to get other families to join you in your fast and share your experiences.

# Three Pillars of Lent

*Almsgiving*

The third pillar of Lent is almsgiving. Giving to the poor is a key feature of most of the world's religions. In Christianity, giving is especially important during Lent. Almsgiving is one of the three traditional Lenten "pillars," along with prayer and fasting. This practice is modified for families to be an offering of food, rather than money. Food is a tangible thing for young minds to grasp and it also offers an opportunity to talk about hunger in your community.

**Designed for Ages 6+**

**Materials**
1. Large cardboard box
2. Materials for decorating the box: paper, markers, tape, and glue

**Time Investment**
30 minutes to make the box, 1 minute per day for 40 days, and time to deliver the box to the organization receiving the food.

**How To**
1. Before the 40-day period of food collecting is to begin, research a food pantry or nonprofit organization that would welcome 40 food items at the end of your collection period. The best match is an organization that accepts a wide variety of food items. One of the goals of the practice is for children to choose items they enjoy and to think about how these items will benefit others. Be sure to check and bring food items that are useful to the organization.

2. On Ash Wednesday, the first day of Lent, explain to the family that one of the pillars of Lent is to give alms. Alms are a monetary sacrifice to help people in need. Tell your family that your alms will

*Three Pillars of Lent: Almsgiving*

___

be to give one food item per day from your pantry.

3. Decorate the box and label it "The Giving Box." As you are decorating, talk about the practice and how it will work: each day one family member will select something from the pantry to put in the box and, at the end of the 40 days, the box of food will be delivered to the organization that has been selected.

4. For each of the 40 days, take turns putting an item in the box. Choose a time of day to do this that fits into your family routine (at the beginning or end of dinner, first thing in the morning, last thing at the end of the day, etc.) Talk about hunger during this time. How do you feel when you are hungry? If you were hungry every day, what would you pray for?

5. Deliver the food as a family after Lent is over.

**Notes**
- One focus of almsgiving is to give out of our sustenance, not our excess. For this reason I suggest you challenge family members to choose their favorite foods for the box. Try not to "censor" what goes in to the box. If a child chooses a box of cereal that you were planning to use for the weekly breakfasts, challenge yourselves to eat something different for breakfast. If someone chooses a canned good that was needed for supper, go without and talk about how it feels to make changes or sacrifices for others.

- Make sure all food is unopened, unexpired, and is appropriate for the demographic that will receive the food.

**Variations**
- Find an organization that needs gently used household goods and choose one item from your house per day for 40 days.
- Give money each day for 40 days.

- Take the food weekly instead of storing it up for the entire 40 days.

- Do the activity during any 40-day period of time, not only Lent.

- Try to give one food item per day for an entire year.

# Easter

*Witnessing Resurrection*

When I was in kindergarten, my dad found a butterfly chrysalis in our garden. He talked with the teacher, who agreed it would be a great learning opportunity for our class. The entire class crowded around the chrysalis every day, anxious to see if that would be the day that the butterfly would emerge. Imagine the awe and wonder for our class of five year olds one Monday morning when we walked into class to see a butterfly hanging upside-down in its makeshift habitat, drying its newly emerged wings.

The teacher let me be the one to release the butterfly, and the whole class watched with fascination as it flew away. Butterflies are traditionally a symbol of the Resurrection, as they represent transformation and change. This whimsical activity is a powerful illustration of transformation and resurrection.

**Designed for ages 3+**

**Materials**
Butterfly chrysalis and habitat (see notes for details)

**Time Investment:** 7–10 days of waiting, 30 minutes of discussion

**How To**
1. Approximately 10 days before Easter, order a butterfly chrysalis and habitat from a reputable company. (See notes.)

2. When the chrysalis arrives, have a short discussion about butterflies and their transformation. Some questions to guide you:

*What is happening inside this chrysalis right now?*

*How are you feeling about it? Excited? Hopeful? Impatient?*

3. Wait for the butterfly to emerge. When it does...celebrate! Use the opportunity for another discussion:

*How does this butterfly remind us of what God is like?*

*How do people change and transform?*

4. When it is time to release the butterfly, release it with these words, *"God, we thank you for teaching us about change and miracles, and we thank you for this butterfly. Help us have a wonderful Easter season. In Jesus' name we pray. Amen."*

**Notes**
- To get the chrysalis and habitat, run an Internet search on "Live butterfly chrysalis." Choose a company that guarantees at least one of the chrysalises will produce a live butterfly.

- More than any other activity in this book, this one requires advance planning, a financial investment, and uncommon materials. That said, the impact of this activity is powerful, and the activity is quite special, just as resurrection is special. Consider alternating this live butterfly activity with some the variations below from year to year.

- Though this activity is timed for the butterfly to emerge around Easter, it is impossible to guarantee this will happen. Instead of being a drawback, this is a benefit, because it provides an opportunity to talk about it. Sometimes the transformation we are expecting to see takes longer than we expect; sometimes it comes early!

*Easter: Witnessing Resurrection*

---

## Variations

- Instead of a live butterfly activity, draw a chrysalis (cocoon) several days before Easter. Then, on Easter, make your own butterfly by drawing one, cutting one out of construction paper, or finding a butterfly craft your family would like to do. Go through the discussion questions above.

- Search for instructions on an origami butterfly or other crafty butterfly. Make a variety of butterflies and hang them in your home to remember the Resurrection.

# Easter

*Have a Family Sunrise Breakfast*

Getting up before dawn to watch the sunrise is a special treasure that is not easily forgotten in life. This Easter morning tradition of a sunrise breakfast creates a sacred space in which memories are cultivated for life. Some families already have this tradition and gather together in community for a sunrise service. For those who don't, however, why not do it at home? Breakfast can be as simple or elaborate as you wish. The most important element is simply gathering together as a family and enjoying the time together.

**Designed for All Ages**

**Materials**

1. Breakfast foods

2. Printout of John chapter 20:1–18 (a link to the printout is available at www.traci-smith.com/resources)

**Time Investment:** 1 hour

**How To**

1. The night before, set the table. If possible, consider setting up outside on a balcony or deck, or near a window to see the sunrise. Also, prepare as much of breakfast ahead of time as possible as well.

2. Plan to wake everyone in time to be ready at the table about 10–15 minutes before sunrise.

3. Serve breakfast and have everyone seated. Begin with a prayer of your own or use this one: *"God of darkness and light, we give you thanks for this Easter morning. As we sit here in the dark, we are*

## Easter: Have a Family Sunrise Breakfast

*excited to experience resurrection in a new way as the sun rises and light fills the sky. Help us to have a meaningful breakfast together as a family. Amen."*

4. Begin to eat breakfast together and have someone read the John passage slowly and deliberately.

5. Notice the first line: "Early on the first day of the week, while it was still dark…" (20:1a, NRSV). Notice if it is still dark outside, and notice that this is how it was outside when Mary went to the tomb. Ask *"How do you think Mary felt when she went to the tomb in the dark?"* If you are able to eat outside, notice what sounds you hear. Is it quiet? Is it noisy?

6. Enjoy breakfast together and notice as it gets brighter and day breaks. Share any thoughts and experiences that come to mind. Ask questions that occur to you or use one (or more) of the following:

- *What part of the story is most interesting to you or sticks out the most?*

- *Does the light happen all at once, or does it seem to get light outside gradually? What does this tell us about the resurrection?*

- *In the story, Mary calls Jesus a teacher. How is Jesus a teacher to you?*

- *How do you think people felt when they realized that Jesus was alive?*

- *Resurrection means coming back to life. What are some things that remind you of resurrection in the world?*

7. Close your time together with a prayer: "Thank you, God, for this resurrection breakfast, a time to focus on you and the mystery of resurrection. Help us to celebrate Easter and to share its message of hope and promise. Amen."

**Notes**
- Parents and grandparents often complain to me how commercialized Easter has become. The focus seems to be more and more on gifts, bunnies, eggs, and chocolate. Certainly, families can choose to engage some of the secular Easter traditions as much or as little as they would like. The beauty of this tradition, though, is that it starts the morning with a spiritual focus and centers the day in family and faith.

- This tradition is a great foundation on which to build other traditions as the years go on. Add your own special recipes and surprises at breakfast.

**Variations**
- Use different scriptures and readings in different years.

- Add different songs, scriptures, or other readings that are meaningful to your family.

- Use this breakfast as a time to reflect on any of the other practices from this book that your family has been practicing together.

# Earth Day

*Feeding the Birds*

Children often show a special sensitivity to the earth and God's creatures. This practice is designed to help children honor creation every year on Earth Day by reading the creation story and making a bird feeder. The creation stories in Genesis chapters one and two tell of the beauty of all God has made: the day and the night, the water and the land, the plants and the animals. Birds are a symbol throughout scripture of God's provision for God's people. They are a symbol of new life and hope. This is a simple practice of caring for God's creation by making a simple bird feeder for your home.

**Designed for Ages 4+**

**Materials**

1. Pipe cleaners

2. O-shaped cereal

**Time Investment: 10–15 Minutes**

**How To**

1. Gather everyone together outside with the needed supplies.

2. Read Genesis 1.

3. Choose one or more of the following questions to discuss with your family:

  • *What is your favorite part of creation?*

  • *When God created the world, God used the word good to describe it. What other words would you use to describe God's creation?*

- *Look around our yard; what are some of the things that God created here? What animals or plants do you notice?*

- *Today is Earth Day, a day to think about how we might protect our planet and environment. God also says that human beings are to be good stewards of the earth. What are some of the things we can do to protect and honor the earth that God has made?*

4. Make the bird feeder by stringing "o" cereal on a pipe cleaner and bending it into a ring.

5. Place the bird feeder on the tree, saying, *"Thank you, God, for creating the world and giving us plants and animals. Help us to do our part to take care of your creation. Amen."*

**Notes**
- Birds are present throughout scripture in a variety of different stories. For teens and older children, consider looking up references of birds in scripture. Examples:

- The dove returning to Noah's ark with the olive sprig (Genesis 8)

- Quails in the desert (Exodus 16:11, 13)

- Ravens bringing food to Elijah (1 Kings 17:6)

- The dove at Jesus' baptism (Matthew 3:13-17)

- Many different faiths have creation myths that are similar to the Judeo-Christian story. Consider researching other stories to help

*Earth Day: Feeding the Birds*

---

children understand how their story is similar and different to the stories of other faiths.

**Variations**

- Search for other bird feeder designs that might be more appealing to older children. There are plenty of instructions online for feeders that attract different types of birds. See www.traci-smith.com/resources for links.

- Make a bird bath instead of a feeder.

- Do something in your home or neighborhood to clean up your environment: pick up trash, participate in a river or forest clean-up, or learn about your city's efforts to reduce waste.

# Pentecost

*Harness the Power of the Wind*

Pentecost is the day when Christians remember the Holy Spirit coming into the world. Start a tradition with your family of flying a kite on or near the day of Pentecost. If you are able to invest in a higher quality kite made of fabric, it can be used from year to year. This tradition creates a memorable connection between the Spirit and wind. Imagine the powerful effect it would have on your children if they thought of the power of the Holy Spirit each time they saw a colorful kite flying in the sky!

**Designed for All Ages**

**Materials**
1. A red kite with string (the color is optional)
2. A windy day

**Time Investment:** 30 minutes—2 hours

**How To**
1. The first year, present the family with a kite on the day of Pentecost. Since red is the traditional liturgical color for Pentecost, selecting a red kite further connects the idea of liturgical colors. (See "Color Your Year" in the previous chapter.)

2. Travel to an open space and fly the kite. As the kite flies, talk about the connection between the Spirit and the wind. Though we cannot see the wind, we see the effect of the wind as it props up the kite and helps it to fly. The same is true with the Spirit: we cannot see it, yet we see evidence of the Spirit's work and movement among us as we help others in need, as others help us, as we pray, and as we worship.

*Pentecost: Harness the Power of the Wind*

---

3. Take turns flying the kite and watching it fly higher and higher.

**Notes**

- If your family flies a kite often, consider using a separate Pentecost kite just for this occasion.

- While younger toddlers and babies are too little to fly the kite themselves, they can still benefit from the joy of being outside in the breeze and watching the kite fly. Why not fly a kite with baby, too?

- Because weather does not always cooperate, the family tradition might need to be approximately the time of Pentecost rather than the actual day.

**Variations**

- Make your own kite and draw or paint a symbol of the Holy Spirit on it.

- Maintain a similar tradition with a windsock that is hung outside each year around Pentecost time.

# Thanksgiving

*Gratitude Tree*

Cultivating a spirit of gratitude has proven to lower stress and lead people toward a more optimistic worldview and greater life satisfaction. What better day to cultivate a spirit of gratitude than Thanksgiving? Thanksgiving is not a religious holiday, but it is a perfect day to focus on our blessings. This version of a gratitude tree is simplified in that it makes use of a tree you already have growing rather than having you craft one.

**Designed for Ages 5+**

**Materials**
1. Construction paper
2. Scissors
3. Hole punch
4. Markers/crayons/pencils
5. Yarn
6. A tree (or bush) in the yard with branches low enough to hang ornaments from

**Time Investment:**
15–45 minutes for the activity, plus time to make the gratitude ornaments

**How To**
1. Cut out construction paper circles, punch a hole in each of them, and tie a loop of yarn through each hole. This will create the circle ornaments that can hang on the tree. Make enough circle ornaments for each family member to have at least three.

2. On Thanksgiving Day, before or after the meal, ask each family member to sit at the table and write down on the ornaments at least

*Thanksgiving: Gratitude Tree*

---

three reasons he or she is thankful (one reason per ornament). Younger children can draw pictures. Remind everyone that the reasons will be shared.

3. Gather outside at the tree.

4. Take turns naming the items and hanging them on the tree.

5. After the conclusion of the tradition, someone says, *"Our tree is full of so many reasons why we are grateful this day. Let us continue our celebration together knowing that our lives are full! Let's all say AMEN!"*

6. Invite everyone to take their ornaments home with them.

**Notes**

- It is easy for some people to think of things that they are grateful for. It's more of a challenge for others. Help those who need a little assistance by prompting. Is there anyone in this house you are thankful for? What about the food you eat or the clothes you wear?

- Try not to evaluate what people (particularly children) list on their gratitude ornaments. A child might want to be grateful for her toys, her video games, and her puzzles instead of the bed she sleeps in, the food she eats, and the clothes she wears. The exercise is about naming things that we are grateful for, not inspiring guilt.

**Variations**

- Create an indoor tree by putting a large branch in a tall vase.

- Make the gratitude ornaments shaped like leaves.

- Do the exercise on a different fall day.

# Advent

*Make and Use an Advent Wreath*

Many Protestant and Roman Catholic churches use Advent wreaths to mark the passing of the four weeks in Advent. The candles are lit, one additional one per week, for four weeks. Often a special liturgy accompanies the lighting of the candle. In this version for the home, the family gathers around a very simple votive wreath to have dessert together and talk about each of the four Advent candles: hope, peace, joy, and love. On Christmas Eve, a fifth candle is lit to represent Christ, the light of the world.

**Designed for Ages 4+**

**Materials**
1. Four votive candles: these are the weekly candles that represent hope, peace, joy, and love

2. One pillar candle: this is the Christmas Eve candle that represents Christ, the light of the world

3. A plate large enough to accommodate all five candles

4. Special dessert: candy canes, hot cocoa, cookies, ice cream, etc.

**Time Investment**
5 minutes to put the wreath together, and 15 minutes each week during Advent

**How To**
1. Arrange the votive candles in a circle around the perimeter of the plate.

2. Place the pillar candle in the center.

*Advent: Make and Use an Advent Wreath*

---

**Light The Candles:**
1. Decide which day and time the candles will be lit during Advent. Choose a consistent time for each of the four weeks.

2. Gather everyone together with the special dessert.

3. Light the candle of the corresponding week (as well as the candles from the previous week[s]) and follow the readings below. Take turns reading and lighting the candle(s) from week to week. Candles can remain lit for the evening until the last adult goes to bed.

*Week 1 - Hope:* The leader says, *"This is the first week in Advent, and we light the candle of hope."* The leader lights the first candle, and asks, *"What does it mean to have hope as we wait for Jesus' birth?"*

Everyone takes turns answering the question while enjoying the dessert. Family members can take the conversation wherever it leads. At the conclusion of the sharing time, someone says, *"Let us leave with hope in our hearts."*

*Week 2 - Peace:* The leader lights the first candle and then says, *"This is the second week in Advent. Last week we lit the candle for hope. This week we light the candle of peace."* The leader lights the second candle, and asks, *"What does it mean to have peace as we wait for Jesus' birth?"*

Everyone takes turns answering the question while enjoying the dessert. Family members can take the conversation wherever it leads. At the conclusion of the sharing time, someone says, *"Let us leave with hope and peace in our hearts."*

*Week 3 - Joy:* The leader lights the first two candles and then says, *"This is the third week in Advent. We have already lit the candles for hope and peace, and today we light the candle of joy."* The leader lights the third candle, and asks, *"What does it mean to have joy as we wait for Jesus' birth?"*

Everyone takes turns answering the question while enjoying the dessert. Family members can take the conversation wherever it leads. At the conclusion of the sharing time, someone says, *"Let us leave with hope, peace, and joy in our hearts."*

*Week 4 - Love:* The leader lights the first three candles and then says, *"This is the fourth week in Advent. We have already lit the candles for hope, peace, and joy, and today we light the candle of love."* The leader lights the fourth candle, and asks, *"What does it mean to have love as we wait for Jesus' birth?"*

Everyone takes turns answering the question while enjoying the dessert. Family members can take the conversation wherever it leads. At the conclusion of the sharing time, someone says, *"Let us leave with hope, peace, joy and love in our hearts."*

*Christmas Eve:* The leader lights the votive candles and says, *"Tonight is Christmas Eve. We have already lit candles for hope, peace, joy, and love, and we have talked about what it means to have these things as we wait for Jesus' birth. Today we celebrate the coming of Christ into the world and we light the Christ candle."* The leader lights the Christ candle, and asks, *"As we think about Christmas, how do we experience the hope, peace, joy, and love of Jesus in our lives?"* Conclude the Christmas Eve sharing time by singing "Silent Night" and saying Merry Christmas to one another.

## *Advent: Make and Use an Advent Wreath*

---

### Notes

- In some churches, three of the candles are blue or purple and one (the joy candle) is pink. If this is the tradition in your church, consider doing the same at home.

- This tradition grounds Advent in a spiritual realm, which is in stark contrast to the glitzy consumerism all around during this time of year. It's nice to take a moment to think about how the values of hope, peace, joy, and love contrast with the values of shopping, buying, wrapping, and doing that our culture often holds in esteem.

- The questions for each week are deliberately simple, open-ended, and repetitive. If the response is thin the first year, remind family members that next year the same questions will be asked. They might have more to say the next year.

### Variations

- Think of your own questions about hope, peace, love, and joy, and use them during the question time.

- If your church does an Advent candle lighting, discuss the readings from church during your home celebration.

- Make a more elaborate wreath and involve the family. Some ideas include: using evergreen leaves, making a wire wreath, or decorating the candles with ribbon.

- Use battery-operated candles for safety when appropriate.

# Advent

*Make an Acts of Kindness Tree*

Whereas the liturgical season of Advent is focused on quiet reflection and waiting, the wider culture is focused on buying and consuming. How can parents take the lead in helping their families focus on values of kindness, service, and giving during such a busy time of year? Make an "acts of kindness tree" that helps to bring focus to the season.

**Designed for Ages 5+**

**Materials**
1. Acts of kindness ornaments (visit www.traci-smith.com/ resources for a link to printable ornaments, or make your own using the suggestions in the "how to" section)

2. Small Christmas tree or branch that will be dedicated to this purpose

**Time Investment:** Varies

**How To**
1. Make 25 acts of kindness ornaments for your advent tree. Visit www.traci-smith.com/resources for a link to a printable template you can buy, or make your own ornaments. To make your own, cut out 25 shapes (stars, bells, candy canes, etc.) and write the 25 following instructions on them (one per ornament).

> *1. Give someone a compliment.*
> *2. Feed the birds.*
> *3. Write someone a thank-you note.*
> *4. Leave an encouraging note around the house for someone to see.*

*Advent: Make an Acts of Kindness Tree*

---

*5. Pick up trash around your house or school.*

*6. Do a chore for someone (set the table, sweep the floor, or take out the trash).*

*7. Tell someone in your family why he or she is important to you.*

*8. Send a card to someone who needs extra love.*

*9. Donate food to the food pantry.*

*10. Make a homemade gift for someone.*

*11. Smile at everyone you see today.*

*12. Do something kind for a neighbor (bring their garbage cans up to their house, shovel or sweep their driveway, bring over a treat or gift).*

*13. Pass on a book or toy to a friend.*

*14. Hold the door open for someone.*

*15. Leave some pennies (heads up) on the sidewalk to wish someone a happy day.*

*16. Think of five things you are grateful for and share them with your family.*

*17. Let someone go ahead of you in line.*

*18. Bring flowers or cookies to a nursing home or hospital.*

*19. Tell your postal worker that he or she is doing a good job.*

*20. Tidy up your room (or a common area) without being asked.*

*21. Pray for a country that is far away from your country.*

*22. Take a photo of something beautiful and share it with someone in your family.*

*23. Draw a picture or write a poem for someone else.*

*24. Find little ways to help the planet, such as turning off unnecessary lights or using less water.*

*25. Spend time with family or friends instead of watching TV or other electronics.*

2. Once the ornaments are made, place them on a tree or branch.

3. Take an ornament off the tree each day and do the act of kindness it suggests.

4. Repeat step 3 each day.

**Notes**

- The ornaments can be numbered prior to placement on the tree. If this is done, consider looking at the calendar and placing more challenging activities on the days that are less occupied for your family, and easier activities on busy days.

- There is a danger in this activity becoming "just one more thing" to do during Advent. I advise a spirit of flexibility and grace for this activity. If your family isn't able to complete an activity one day, no worries. Pick it up the next day, after Christmas, or simply let it go.

**Variations**

- Put ornaments in a basket or box instead of on a tree.

- Do activities at random (or on selected days only) rather than one per day.

- Do this activity at a different time of year, instead of only Advent.

# A Christmas Tree Blessing

This tradition allows families to bring a moment of spirituality to the secular tradition of decorating the tree. Try having a different family member read the blessing each year.

**Designed for All Ages**

**Time Investment:** 1—2 minutes

**Materials**
1. Blessing (printed below)
2. Christmas Tree (before decorating)
3. Manger scene / crèche scene (optional)

**How To**
1. Before the tree is decorated, gather everyone together and read the following blessing:

*God who created the birds in the air, the fish in the sea, the stars in the sky, and the trees in the ground, bless this tree as we decorate it and make it a joyful symbol in our home. May its branches remind us of the shade and shelter you provide for us and for many creatures. May its trunk remind us of your strength. May its lights bring us peace. May we remember your gift to us this season, the gift of the baby Jesus. Amen.*

2. Optional (see note below)—After decorating the tree, set up a crèche or manger scene below the tree.

**Note**
- In the United States, there seems to be a sharp division between secular Christmas traditions (the tree, the stockings, Santa) and

Christian traditions (the manger scene, attending church, singing Christmas carols). As the tree is the focal point in many homes during Christmas, blessing the tree and setting up a manger scene under the tree (as opposed to gifts) can highlight the Christian significance of the day, something culture has lost sight of.

**Variations**

- Print the blessing on an ornament and say it as the ornament is hung on the tree.

- Write a new blessing each year and collect them from year to year.

- Cut down your own tree and say this blessing before the tree is cut down and brought home.

- Adapt the language of the blessing to the age of your children or your own traditions and culture.

# Birthday

*A Gift of Self to Others*

The women of the Presbyterian Church (USA), my denominational home, have an offering called The Birthday Offering. Women are encouraged to donate money to organizations supported by the Presbyterian Women and to use their birthdays as the motivation. It is suggested that each woman give the number of dollars that matches her age. Those birthday offerings inspire this tradition. In this variation, children give a toy to someone else as a reminder that birthdays are an opportunity to celebrate life by giving something to others.

**Designed for Ages 5 and up**

**Materials**
A gift

**Time Investment**
10 minutes of discussion, plus time to choose (or buy) a toy and drive to a place it will be of use

**How To**
1. In advance of the child's birthday, parents or caregivers should do some research on local nonprofit organizations that are accepting new or gently used toys for children. If you need help finding a good charity, use the Internet or the help of a pastor or teacher.

2. Explain to children that each year on their respective birthdays, they will have the opportunity to give thanks for their lives by giving a toy to another child.

3. Encourage the birthday child to pick out a toy to give away that another child will really love. Alternatively, have the child use his or

her allowance or other birthday money to purchase a toy for another child.

4. Take the toy to your selected organization. If possible, arrange to have a tour of the organization or to hear a little about its work.

**Notes**

• It is crucial that a parent guide the child through this exercise by encouraging the joy of giving. Children must not be allowed to give away toys that are broken, dirty, or damaged. If it is a toy that has outlived its usefulness for the birthday child, this is fine, but the emphasis should be made on how much joy the toy brought when the child played with it. If a toy is being purchased for this activity, resist the temptation to provide the money out of the parents' pockets. This is the child's gift and sacrifice.

• It helps to have a special relationship with the organization that will be the recipient of this gift. Some organizations might be burdened by taking the time to receive just one toy (especially if they don't have advance notice). Take advantage of any personal connections you have and try and find someone who will take the time to understand what your children are doing and how they are growing in their sense of sharing.

• Some children are naturally more generous and take to activities like this easier than others. One child might feel inspired to give away a beloved toy or to use an entire allowance for this purpose, while another struggles to give away even a small toy. Recognize their differences and resist the urge to compare or push too hard. As long as there is an insistence that toys be in good shape and clean, the offering should be praised.

*Birthday: A Gift of Self to Others*

- Parents should follow this tradition as well, though their "toys" are certainly different! Model some of what a child might be thinking when it is your turn. *"It was hard for me to give away those pretty dishes, but I was so happy to think about someone using the gift that I gave them on my birthday!"*

**Variations**

- Give away an entire box of toys each birthday.

- Invite children to a party where all of the gifts given will be donated to a charity.

- Allow a child to earn money in advance of his/her birthday for this purpose. Encourage a donation of one dollar for each year of life.

# Birthday

*Celebrate the Giver*

I have a very clear memory of being about 10 years old and receiving a piece of clothing from my grandmother that I thought was dreadful. I looked my grandma in the eye and said thank you and smiled. The most profound moment was when my mother took me aside later and said, "I know you didn't like that gift, and I'm so proud of you for not saying anything and for being gracious." I remember being proud, too, and even happy with the clothes, knowing that my grandma had thought of me. Learning to be a gracious receiver is a skill, to be learned just like eating with a fork or playing soccer. This practice is among the most simple in the book and requires no more than a sentence or two before opening a gift. I got this idea from a reader who shared it at a workshop on family faith practices. Thank you, kind reader!

**Designed for All Ages**

**Materials**
None

**Time Investment:** Less than 1 minute

**How To**
When you or your children are at a birthday party and there are multiple givers and multiple presents, the birthday honoree opens each gift in front of everyone and says, *"This gift is from* [giver's name] *and one thing I love about* [him/her] *is that* [tell a quality or trait about that person]."

**Notes**
• There is a trend in some parts of the country for children to not open their gifts in front of their peers at birthday parties. I don't know how

## Birthday: Celebrate the Giver

or why it started, but I think it's a mistake. Children learn the joy of giving when they see their friend's reaction at a party. Additionally, the birthday child has the joy (and responsibility) of thanking the giver in a situation like this. Though it seems to be countercultural in some places, I encourage parents to allow children to open presents at birthday parties. It's good for everyone!

- For some children, especially young children or those who aren't as comfortable speaking out in a group, this exercise might take practice at home. Practice what to say, knowing who will be present.

- This practice is not limited to children! Parents should model it as well.

### Variations
- Try this practice on Christmas or other occasions, not just birthdays.

- When there is one giver, leave out the, *"This gift is from* [giver's name]," and simply say, *"Thank you so much for this gift. I really appreciate how you* [trait or quality about the person]."

- Change the words and use a different script of your own choosing.

# Remembering Our Baptism

*A Part of God's Family Too*

This tradition allows family members to celebrate their baptisms annually through a short liturgy. In the Reformed tradition, in which I was raised and am now ordained as a minister, we believe in infant baptism. Though infants cannot make their own statements of faith, they are baptized into the community of faith as a reminder of God's covenant promises to us. God chooses us and claims us even before we are aware of God. Though there are many Christians who practice infant baptism, there are also a great many who practice a believer's baptism instead. This tradition is appropriate in both contexts. For those who practice infant baptism, the tradition can begin as early as four years old.

### Designed for Ages 4+ or after the Age of Baptism

### Materials
1. Small bottle of water
2. Pictures of baptism/baptismal celebrations (optional)
3. Cake

**Time Investment:** 10 minutes

### How To
1. Begin by saying, *"For each of us the day of our baptism was a very special day. Though we are a part of our own family sitting here, we are also a part of God's family. Today we are going to remember this important part of our journey of faith."*

2. If family members were baptized as infants say , *"Since we were babies when we were baptized, we don't remember it, but we know that even then, God had chosen us and made us a part of God's family."*

*Remembering Our Baptism: A Part of God's Family Too*

_____

3. Continue, *"Water is an important symbol in the Bible. God created the water; Moses parted the Red Sea; Jesus was baptized with water. Baptism with water is a symbol of our new life with Jesus. When we were baptized we were baptized with water."*

4. Tell stories about the children's baptisms or ask them to tell stories about their experiences (if they were old enough to remember). If you have pictures of that day, share them at this point.

5. Conclude the liturgy portion of the tradition by taking turns making the sign of the cross on one another's palms with the water. Say, *"[Name], remember your baptism, and be thankful."* Everyone says, *"Amen."*

6. Celebrate by having cake!

**Notes**
- Consider using water that is somehow special to your family's faith journey. For example, if the family has the opportunity to visit the Jordan River where Jesus was baptized, take home water from it or bring home the water from the day of your child's baptism.

- The reason family members make the sign of the cross on each other's hands rather than foreheads is to emphasize the difference between the actual moment of baptism and this, the remembrance of it.

**Variations**
- Put rocks in a bowl of water, and ask each family member to reach in and draw out a rock to remember his or her baptism.

- Celebrate one person's baptism each year. Alternate who is celebrated from year to year.

# Part Two

---

# Ceremonies

# Chapter 3

*Ceremonies for Marking Life's Transitions*

# Garland of Hopes for a New Baby

When a new baby comes into the family, it is important not only to affirm the older children in the home, but to also begin to talk about how life will change when the baby arrives. Creating a garland of hopes provides the opportunity to do both, and the end product can be displayed over the new baby's crib.

**Designed for Ages 2+**
(See modifications for younger children in the "how to" portion)

**Materials**
1. Eight to ten large paper circles in different colors. Pre-cut these if your older children are still only toddlers, or have your school-age children cut them out as a part of the ceremony. Punch a hole in the top of each circle.
2. Yarn or ribbon
3. Markers or crayons
4. Scissors

**Time Investment:** 30 minutes—1 hour

**How To**
1. In about the seventh month of Mom's pregnancy, parents sit older child(ren) down and tell them that it is time to prepare for the new baby's birth, and that to do this, you have a very special project you will all do together.

2. Begin by telling the children that before they were a part of your family, you talked a lot about the hopes you had for them. You had hope that they would be safe and well. You had hope that they would always know God's love. You had hope that they would always be safe from harm. You had hope that they would be happy and kind

children. Remind them that you still have many hopes for them, and you always will.

3. Explain that you will make a garland of hopes for the new baby, writing down (or drawing) on the paper circles the things you hope will happen for the new baby. Parents can start by writing down an example of their own. When you are done with all the circles, string them on the ribbon and hang it over the new baby's crib.

**Notes**
- If the concept of "hopes" is too abstract for your young child, encourage him or her to draw a picture of what the new baby might look like, or a picture of your new family with the baby included.

- Use the time to also highlight your older children's special characteristics. Tell the stories of their births or adoptions, and remind them that the new baby will not replace them.

- If a new baby is coming into your family via adoption, do this activity a few weeks into the waiting process, and explain to your children that you don't know exactly when the new baby will come. (See "Waiting," in chapter 7.)

**Variations**
- Instead of using paper circles with words, cut out pictures of things that represent the hopes you have and string those together instead.

- Make a booklet instead of a garland.

# Welcoming a New Pet to the Family

*Promising to Care for One of God's Creatures*

Bringing a pet into the home is a great joy and responsibility. Many animal lovers agree: pets have a very special place in the family's life. Having a pet in the house is an excellent opportunity for children to practice disciplines of patience, compassion, and kindness. This welcome ceremony centers around the idea of identity and belonging. To whom does the pet belong? Although the pet has been entrusted to the family's care, the pet ultimately belongs to God, who created all living things.

**Designed for Ages 5+**

**Materials**
1. Pet ID tag or equivalent (see notes for details)
2. Camera with timer function (optional)

**Time Investment:** 15 minutes

**How To**
1. On the day the pet is brought home (or after he or she has a name), everyone gathers together for the welcome ceremony. Begin by saying, *"Today is a very special day for our family because we welcome [pet's name] into our lives. [Name] is not a human being, of course, but [he/she] is very precious in God's sight. God created the world and everything in it, and God created [name] too."*

2. Say, *"We are going to put on [name's] collar now. Even though our family's address is on it, we know that [he/she] belongs to God most of all, and we have been trusted to take care of [him/her]."*

3. Continue, saying, *"I will put the collar on [name], but we will all have a chance to welcome [him/her]."* Put the collar on the pet and

say, *"Welcome to our family, [pet's name]. God bless you."* Invite each family member to touch the pet and say the same thing: *"Welcome to our family. God bless you."*

4. Finish by setting up the camera and taking a picture of the whole family with the pet to remember this special moment.

**Notes**
- This ceremony assumes that the pet will have an identification tag. For animals that do not have identification collars (birds, fish, etc.), get some sort of tag made up anyway for this ceremony. It can be attached to a cage or aquarium, and it serves as a powerful symbol.

- Because the pet is so new to the family, it might be necessary for family members not to touch the pet. Use your discretion and the advice of your vet or other experts. If it might be too much activity for your pet to have many hands touching and blessing him or her, still take turns saying the welcome and blessing.

**Variations**
- Conclude the welcome ceremony with a party or special treats for animals and humans alike.

- Present the pet with gifts that will help him or her feel welcome in the new house.

- Ask each family member to say one reason they are thankful for or excited about the new pet.

- Put *"God Bless [pet's name]"* on the reverse side of the ID tag, or get a separate tag with that inscription to go alongside the address tag.

# Starting a New Journey

*Moving*

There is a wonderful Buddhist parable called, *The Parable of the Raft.* The basic plot is this: a person is on a journey and builds a raft to cross a dangerous stream. After crossing it, the traveler feels grateful to the raft for its protection and so she carries the raft on her back in case it is needed again. After awhile, though, it becomes clear that the burden of the raft is too heavy; the raft must be laid down to continue. The traveler takes a stick from the raft as a memory, puts it in her pocket and continues on. So it is with the homes we inhabit: they are meaningful and precious to us, but we have to leave them behind.

**Designed for Ages 5+**

**Materials**
A photo of the house or apartment that you are moving from

**Time Investment:** 10 minutes

**How To**
1. Pick a meaningful time on moving day to gather everyone together —either early in the morning before the chaos begins or after every-thing has been packed up and the house is empty.

2. Have someone in the family tell a kid-friendly version of the parable of the raft. If there is a good storyteller in the house, he or she can tell it with details that are meaningful to the family. Alternately, do an Internet search of, *The Parable of the Raft* and adopt the language of some of the great storytellers.

3. Have someone in your family say, *"In the story, the traveler might have really wanted to take the raft with her, but she had to let it go. In*

*the same way, we have to leave this house and we can't take it with us. In the story, the traveler took a stick with her to remind her of the raft. We are going to take a picture of the old house with us when we move."* Show the picture.

4. Take turns sharing one favorite thing about the old house.

5. Conclude with a prayer: *"God, we thank you for our house and all the happy memories we had living here. Help us to have happy memories in our new house as well. Amen."*

6. Put the picture in a prominent place in the new house.

**Note**
- Depending on the circumstances of your move, this activity has the potential to be emotional or teary. If this is likely to be the case, be prepared to tell children that it's okay to be sad, and being sad is a reminder of how much you cared about the house. Use the story for inspiration. *"I'm sure the traveler was very sad to leave the raft behind, too."* Be sure to leave plenty of time if you sense your family will want to share many memories.

**Variations**
- Make a longer activity and travel from room to room telling stories about memories that happened there.

- Ask family members to draw or paint a picture of the house, and share it at this time. Frame it in the new house.

- If your family has to move a lot, you can take turns telling the story each time you move, and collect the photos or drawings in an album.

# Bless the New Driver

*A Ceremony upon Getting a License*

When a teenager passes the important milestone of getting a driver's license, concerned parents and family members often have a lot to say in worry: *Don't drive too fast! Remember to wear your seat belt! No texting and driving!* This ceremony reminds the newly licensed that God loves and cares about him or her, and offers a symbol of that love and care in a way that is positive and affirming, and also recognizes the exciting milestone of learning to drive.

## Designed for Ages 16+

### Materials
1. Puffy paint
2. Wax paper

### Time Investment
To make the window cling: 10 minutes of active time, 24 hours of drying time; for the ceremony: 20–30 minutes

### How to
### *Make a Heart-Shaped Window Cling*
1. Draw a small outline (2–4 inches wide) of a heart with puffy paint on a piece of wax paper

2. Fill the heart in with a thick layer of the paint

3. Wait at least 24 hours for the paint to dry

### *Bless the New Driver*
1. Tell your teenager that you'd like to have a special meeting—in the car! Invite younger children or significant family members as

well. Ask your teen to sit in the driver's seat. Bring the heart-shaped window cling with you.

2. Tell your child that you are so proud and excited that he has a new driver's license and that, though you may be worried at times about his safety, you know and trust that he will make good choices and do his best to stay safe whenever he is entrusted with the car.

3. Stick the heart-shaped window cling in the lower corner of one of the side windows and tell your child it's meant to be a reminder that your love and God's love will be with her whenever she is driving.

4. Say a short prayer:

*God, we thank you for this exciting new time in [Name's] life. Thank you for the new Driver's License and the extra responsibility that comes with it. Help [Name] and [his/her] passengers to always make wise and safe choices, and protect them from harm. Bless [Name] wherever [she/he] goes, not only today, but all of [his/her] days as well. Amen.*

5. Ask your newly licensed driver to drive the family somewhere for ice cream or dinner or some other special place to celebrate!

**Notes**
- This ceremony is rooted in the assumption that the adolescent getting a license is generally a responsible person and that the parents are confident that she can handle the car on her own. If this isn't the case, wait until your child is ready and use this ceremony to mark the moment when she has earned the privilege of using the car responsibly.

*Bless the New Driver: A Ceremony upon Getting a License*

---

- There are few rites of passage in North American culture. Make a big deal out of this milestone, though it's a scary one for parents!

**Variations**
- Buy a window cling in a heart or other shape

- Do the same ceremony with another type of hanging or decorative object for the car. (Beware that it is not always legal to hang something from the rear view mirror; check local laws or avoid the rear view mirror to be safe.)

- Give the new driver presents that have to do with driving: a new keychain, car wash or gas card, etc.

- Ask each family member to say something special to the new driver.

# Celebrating Parents' Milestone Anniversary

In the hustle and bustle and joy of raising children, it's easy to forget that the parents in the family have their own relationship outside of the parenting relationship. This celebration allows children to be involved in a milestone anniversary in a special way.

This ceremony is perfect for families of all types. For same-sex couples, this ceremony can take on special meaning, given the many ways same-sex couples are often excluded from such rituals. This ceremony is also meaningful for families that are blended due to remarriage or past relationships, helping to solidify the current family relationship in a special way using vows.

**Designed for All Ages**

**Materials**
1. Photos of the wedding
2. A cake or special dessert
3. Bulletins (using the liturgy below as a guide)
4. Symbol of the vows (rings, necklace, bracelet, etc.)

**Time Investment:** 30–90 minutes

**How To**
1. In advance of the milestone anniversary (whichever year you decide: 5 years, 10 years, 20 years, etc.) invite your family to the special anniversary celebration.

Talk with your spouse about inviting extended family or friends to the gathering, or make it a simple affair with the immediate family. Invitations can be verbal or printed invitations. If they are printed, get the whole family involved in making them.

*Celebrating Parents' Milestone Anniversary*

2. This celebration has three parts: *Memories, Promises,* and *Celebration.* Ahead of time, decide who will lead the various parts of the ceremony. Be sure to choose which vows will be said, either from the suggested vows below or write your own. On the day of the celebration, gather everyone together, with the family in front.

3. Begin with a welcome. Someone from the family welcomes guests and says, *"Our celebration has three parts. During the memories portion we will share memories and photos of our wedding day. When we do the promises, we will make promises to one another again, just as we did on that special day. Finally, we'll all gather to celebrate with dessert!"*

4. *Memories:* One of the parents (or a designated person who was at the wedding) says, *"I'll start out by sharing one memory of that special day, and then [Dad, Mama, other person present who was there] will continue. We'll continue sharing memories for a few minutes, and also pictures. If you have any questions about that day, ask them!"*

Memories are shared for a time, and the designated person concludes by saying, *"Thank you, God, for these happy memories. Now let's move to our time of promises."*

5. *Promises:* One of the parents (but different from the person in #4) says, "One of the important things we did on that special day was make promises to each other. We are going to make promises again. The children will also have a chance to make a promise. We will end by making a family promise that we will say together." Take turns saying the vows. Conclude with the family promise, said by everyone.

### Parents to Each Other

Option #1: *I, [name], make these promises to you, [name], my [spouse/ husband/wife/partner]. I promise to continue to be your friend and helper, your equal and your co-parent. I promise to say I'm sorry when I make mistakes and to forgive you when you make mistakes. I promise to work hard at our relationship when times are tough, and to give thanks to God when things are good. This I promise before our family and God.*

Option #2: *[Name], to you I renew all of the promises I made on our wedding day, to lift you up when you are down, to cheer you up when you are sad, and to be the type of person you can trust and depend on.*

Option #3: *On this day, our [number of years] anniversary, I promise you, [name], that I will continue to care for you and love you for as many more years as God gives us to be together. I will ask you for help when I need it and offer to help you when I see you are struggling. I love you yesterday, today, and forever.*

### Children to Parents

Option #1: *We promise to remember the special bond our parents have and to do what we can to support their love and friendship. We are thankful that God gave them to each other, and we pray for God's blessing upon them for many more years.*

Option #2: *We promise to respect our parents and remember their love for one another and for us. We will pray for them and give them our blessing today, tomorrow, and every day.*

Option #3: *On this day we are witnesses to promises our parents made before we were born. Today we promise to help them remember*

## Celebrating Parents' Milestone Anniversary

---

*all of the important things about that day so that they can remember all the ways God has blessed them in the past, the present, and the future.*

### Family Promise (all say in unison)

Option #1: *We promise to love and support each other as a family, to remember how God is with us in good times and bad times, happy times and sad times. We promise to love each other and forgive each other.*

Option #2: *We are a family. We promise to remember how God loves and cares for us and to support and love each other no matter what circumstances may come our way. We give thanks to God for everything that God has given us.*

Option #3: *On this special day, we stand before God and our friends to make promises to one another. We promise to love, respect, and care for each other through all that life has to offer. We promise to stand side by side with one another in love and friendship—not only today, but every day.*

6. *Celebration:* At the conclusion of the promises, a family members says, *"Now we will end our celebration of [Mom and Dad's / Mom and Mama's / Mom and Jeff's / Papa and Daddy's / other] service by having cake and ice cream. Let's go to the kitchen and celebrate this wonderful day!"*

### Notes

- For the memories portion: for a larger family or if there are many guests, photos can be projected on the wall or large screen using a computer (or DVD player) and projector for all to see.

- The vows can be read as is, or modified to include important details for your family. You will notice that the language in them is simple so that even small children can begin to grasp their significance. Adults will find the simplicity meaningful as well. Sometimes our most profound promises can be boiled down to simple terms.

**Variations**
- If parents did not have a formal wedding, the memory time can refer to another time. Some examples are: when parents first met, had their first date, decided to be committed to each other, etc.

- Do a variation of this ceremony every year and make it a tradition. During the memory portion, children can learn to tell the story of the wedding day when they have learned enough details from previous years. Make promises specific to the year ahead.

- Have a full dinner, or weave this entire celebration into a sacred meal. (See chapter 6.)

# First Day of School

*New Beginnings*

Heading off to school on the first day can be daunting for parent and child alike, as there are so many questions in one's mind. *"What will the new year be like?" "Will I like my teacher?" "Will my child be happy?"* This is a yearly tradition involving making a copy of your child's footprints on the first day of school and saying a simple prayer for the year to come. This tradition also relates to the graduation ceremony listed next.

**Designed for Ages Preschool—Senior in High School**

**Materials**
1. Construction paper
2. Washable tempera paint
3. Wide paintbrush
4. Shallow pan of soapy water
5. Washcloths and towels

**Time Investment:** 30 minutes

**How To**
1. On the night before or the morning of the first day of school, paint the bottom of your child's feet with a wide paintbrush and ask him or her to step on a piece of construction paper. As he or she does, say,
"Your feet remind us of the journey you will take this year at school. I know that you will learn so many new things and go so many new places. I hope that you will go with courage and strength and know that God goes with you too."

2. Before the child steps off the construction paper, say this short prayer, *"God please be with [child's name] as [he/she] heads off on*

*[his/her] first day of school. May the year be full of new experiences and knowledge, and may [he/she] walk in light and truth every day. Amen."*

3. Wash off the paint from the child's feet and head off to a new year!

**Notes**

- The time investment for this activity is listed at 30 minutes, but it actually takes much less time. The reason for the inflated time is simple: nobody should be rushed on the first day of school! Take the extra time to avoid a stressful morning, or do it the night before.

- Those who are coming to this tradition with older children might be tempted to skip it, thinking, "Well, we haven't done it in the past, we should just skip it." I think it's never too late to start a new tradition, and this is an easy one to start at any time! Go ahead and start it, no matter how old your children are!

**Variations**

- Do handprints instead of footprints.

- Show the footprints from previous years and notice how the child has grown and changed.

- Trace around the hand or foot and make handprints or footprints that way.

- Do this every year on the last day of school instead of the first, and talk about all of the places the child has gone in the past year.

# High School Graduation

*Walking on, in Faith*

### Designed for High School Graduates

### Materials
1. Footprints from the child's first day of school from previous years, or any shoes from when the child was younger (baby shoes, shoes from childhood, sports shoes, etc.). If you haven't saved any, pick up an inexpensive pair of small shoes for purposes of this ceremony.
2. New pair of shoes or a gift card to a shoe store, wrapped and ready to present to the graduate.

### Time Investment: 15 minutes

### How To
1. After graduation, family members of the graduate say, *"Today is a big day for you! I remember when you wore these shoes when you were just a little child, and now you're graduating from high school. In that time you've walked so many places, to kindergarten, fifth grade, middle school, and now high school. We walked together to many classrooms, and we have seen your feet, and every part of you, grow so much!"*

2. Present the gift, saying, *"We have a little token for you now that we'll explain after you open it."*

3. Explain to the graduate that the gift of shoes is to remind her that she will continue to walk her paths into the future with you and God by her side. Though her feet are bigger now, they still have many choices about which way they will go.

4. Conclude with a prayer. *"God, thank you for [graduate's name] and for being with [him/her] every step of the way, from preschool through*

*high school. Please continue to guide [his/her] steps wherever you lead. Amen."*

**Notes**
- If you do not have shoes from the child's younger years and are relying on shoes that you have purchased or borrowed for this purpose, be clear that they aren't the child's actual shoes, but rather that they reminded you of how small her feet were when she was young.

- If parents are divorced, this ceremony can be a powerful time for both parents to come together in sharing these memories and giving this gift. If this is your family's situation, and if it is possible to come together for this moment, it will make a profound statement to your soon-to-be-adult child.

- Many parents have other gifts that they will give their child upon graduation; the shoes, however, are meant to be a part of this ceremony and separate from other gifts.

- This ceremony is designed to go with the first day of school ceremony, also in this chapter. If the family has kept footprints for many years, this is the time to bring them out and look at them as a family.

**Variations**
- Give a pair of shoes that are signed and decorated by family members.

- Put things in the shoes that will be useful for college/beyond (money, gift cards, small trinkets, etc.), or a special letter.

# Moving Out/Going to College

*Taking the Essentials*

This ceremony is for those children who are hardly children anymore—they are going off to college or moving out of the home. We raise our children the best we can, knowing that we fall short, but trusting that God will guide them. We hope and pray that the lessons we have taught them will remain with them always. In this ceremony, family members give the essentials to the one who is leaving: faith, hope, perseverance, gratitude, love, and compassion. Since these things are intangible, they are represented by paper circles, with the word on one side and the message of what is meant on the back.

**Designed for Ages 18+**

**Materials**
1. Construction paper or poster board
2. Markers/pens
3. Scissors

**Time Investment**
10 minutes, plus 30 minutes of advance preparation

**How To**
1. In advance of moving out day / first day of college, all of the family members who are not going away gather together to make the circles. Cut out large circles. On one side write one of the following words:

*Faith, Hope, Perseverance, Gratitude, Compassion, Love.*

On the back, write a little message about the respective quality. You can write how you have seen the child display it in his or her life, what it has meant to you, or a verse from the Bible that emphasizes the quality. Use the ideas below to get you started:

- *Faith* - Faith means trusting in something that you can't see.[4] May you always have faith in your life, even if things get difficult.

- *Hope* - If you have hope, you have everything you need. May you never run out of hope in your life. If you ever feel hopeless, call your family. We are always here for you.

- *Perseverance* - The faithful life is not always easy; sometimes it requires strength to keep going through challenges. We pray God provides you the strength you need day by day to seek and listen to God's voice.

- *Gratitude* - We are so grateful for you! From the time you came into our family, you have been our joy, and you will continue to fill us with many reasons for thanking God. As you move forward in your life, we pray you will take time to be thankful for the many gifts God has given you.

- *Compassion* - You have learned many things in school, but one of the most important lessons in life is the golden rule: Do unto others as you would have them do unto you. We pray you treat others with kindness, remembering that they are made in the image of God, just as you are.

- *Love* - You are so loved! You are loved by your family. You are loved by your friends. Most of all, you are loved by God, who knows everything about you, including the number of hairs on your head. As you take the next step in your life, we pray you feel our love going with you.

*Moving Out / Going to College: Taking the Essentials*

---

2. Decide who will present which circle "gift" on moving out day.

### The Day of the Ceremony

3. On moving out day / first day of college, surprise the child by saying, *"We know you are leaving us, and we are happy for your new adventures, but also sad that you won't be in the house as you have been. We want you to take some very special gifts with you."*

4. Each family member presents his or her gifts by saying, *"I want you to take [name of gift] and [name of other gift] because [explain the reason on the back]."*

5. Conclude by giving a hug and saying a blessing:

*"[Name], may you take with you these essential gifts of faith, hope, perseverance, gratitude, love, and compassion, knowing that God goes with you, and everything you have learned in this family throughout the years goes with you too. Amen."*

### Notes

- The number of circles each family member presents depends on the size of the family and the individual preferences of family members.

- Some family members might choose to write a more detailed note or letter and present that privately to the child who is leaving.

### Variations

- Do the advance preparation and then hide the circles in one of the bags/boxes with an explanation of what they mean.

- Add more circles, and/or change the words to match values that are particularly important to your family.

- Invite key friends/family members to participate as well and give their own gifts. They can either give a completed circle to someone in the immediate family to present, or they can be invited to the ceremony itself.

- Punch a hole in the top of each circle, tie a circle of yarn through each, and place the circles around the child's neck.

# Chapter 4

## *Ceremonies for Difficult Times*

# Illness

*Anointing Our Sick Children*

Anointing is a tradition that spans many centuries and religious traditions, though many people associate it with dying, or an ancient priestly tradition. As a pastor, I have prayed over and anointed many people when they were sick, and often they report feeling a strong sense of peace and calm during and after that sacred moment. There is no reason for parents not to anoint their own children. Anointing reminds children of the connection between body and spirit for healing and wholeness. Sometimes when the body is not well, the spirit has a special opportunity to find peace and refuge.

**Designed for All Ages**

**Materials**
Any kind of oil that won't irritate baby or child's skin. Olive oil and baby oil are two good choices. Avoid special anointing oils. They often contain strong fragrances that can be too harsh for little noses.

**Time Investment:** 1–2 minutes

**How To**
1. When the child is lying in bed, say, *"[Dad/Mom] is going to do a special prayer for healing now."*

2. Read Psalm 23 or a reading of your choice (optional):

The Lord is my shepherd;
I have all that I need.
He lets me rest in green meadows;
He leads me beside peaceful streams.
He renews my strength.
He guides me along right paths,

bringing honor to his name.
Even when I walk through the darkest valley,
I will not be afraid, for you are close beside me.
Your rod and your staff, protect and comfort me.
You prepare a feast for me in the presence of my enemies.
You honor me by anointing my head with oil.
My cup overflows with blessings.
Surely your goodness and unfailing love will pursue
meall the days of my life, and I will live in the
house of the Lord forever (NLT).

3. Put a small amount of oil on your finger (a little goes a long way), make the sign of the cross on the child's head, and say one of the following:

*"[Name], may you have peace in your mind, strength in your body, and hope in your spirit. Amen."*

*"[Name], may you feel better today, and if you can't feel better today, may you feel better tomorrow. Amen."*

*"God Bless [Name] and heal [him/her] from [ailment]. Amen."*

**Notes**
- The connection to be made in this ceremony is the connection between being sick and asking God for healing. But what is healing? Sometimes healing comes to us quickly, sometimes we have to wait, and sometimes it doesn't come at all. When we pray for healing and it doesn't come, we have the opportunity to talk about it with our children. A child may wonder, "Why didn't I get better? We asked God to heal me, but I'm still sick." Instead of shying away from these

*Illness: Anointing Our Sick Children*

---

questions, use them as an opportunity to talk more about it, always remembering, *It is a mystery,* is an appropriate answer many times.

- There is a balance in this ceremony, between doing it all the time for every sniffle, skinned knee, and paper cut, and never doing it, assuming that it should only be done for something serious. One guide we use in our family is to use anointing when an illness or injury is causing suffering that lasts greater than an hour or two.

- What about times and circumstances when the child has a chronic illness that he will live with forever, or a terminal illness he will never recover from? These cases are exponentially much more difficult to manage than the stomach flu, a head cold, or even a broken arm. Still, anointing is a useful and beautiful ceremony even (and especially) in these cases.

- When it is unlikely or impossible, from a medical perspective, that the child will recover, choose the words from the first option on the previous page (or the silent variation below) to emphasize that physical healing is not the only way to wholeness.

**Variations**
- Make the sign of the cross on the child's hand instead of forehead.

- Allow children to anoint parents when they are sick, or for siblings to anoint each other.

- Make the sign of the cross with the oil in silence and say, "Let's have a special prayer for healing. I will put the oil on your forehead and you say your prayer silently. I will pray too."

# Create a Memory Table

*A Ceremony Following the Death of a Loved One*

On November 1 and 2 in Mexico, in connection to All Saint's Day and All Souls Day, most people celebrate the Día de Los Muertos (Day of the Dead). Though the name may sound morbid, at the heart of the celebration is a spirit of remembering those we have lost through death. Central to the day is the creation of altares (altars) in honor of each person. Because of my Protestant background, I use the term "memory table" rather than altar. Certainly each person should use the term that resonates most with their spiritual tradition.

**Designed for Ages 5+**

**Materials**
1. A table or piece of carpet that can be dedicated for this purpose for one or two days
2. Battery-operated or wax candles
3. Items that represent the person being remembered: photos, favorite drink or food, item of clothing, item representing favorite hobbies, etc.

**Time Investment:** 15 minutes—2 hours

**How To**
1. A few days before November 1, explain to children that you will be making a memory table to honor a loved one who has died. Tell them to think about what they would like to put on the table and take suggestions.

2. Gather items for the memory table. On November 1, arrange them on the table together as a family.

*Create a Memory Table: A Ceremony Following the Death of a Loved One*

3. As items are placed on the table, talk about the significance of each item. Tell stories about the person and what you remember most about her. Take the opportunity to remember the person's personality as well as her interests. Was she kind and compassionate? Funny? Disciplined?

4. Light candles and place them on the table to celebrate the light the person brought to the world, and the light of his memory.

**Notes**
- This activity presents an opportunity to talk about death and dying, and about the ways in which people are present to us after we die, though the focus should be on remembrance and life. Ask questions to get the conversation going: How does the person being remembered still live on in your lives? How can you honor the memory of that person?

- If a significant family member has died before the child had the opportunity to know that person personally, make a memory table and use it as an opportunity to teach the child about the significant person. *"You didn't have the chance to meet great-grandma, but she loved peppermints, so that's why we are including them on her table! This is what she looked like."* Leave the table up for a day or two and take a picture of it before taking it down.

**Variations**
- Take turns remembering different people each year. Alternate who gets to choose the person who will be remembered.

- Make a memory book or poster instead of a table.

- Do this activity at a different time of year (not in connection with Día de los Muertos).

# After a Death

*Bubble Prayers*

Though we often think of bubbles floating up and away, in actuality they sink slowly down before they pop. Blow a stream of bubbles and you will see that they fall to the ground like rain, or tears. Bubbles reflect light and color before they are gone. They are fragile and beautiful.

This ceremony uses the qualities of a bubble as an analogy for the many complex emotions a person experiences after a death.

**Designed for Ages 7+**

**Materials**
A small container of bubbles

**Time Investment:** 5 minutes

**How To**
1. Choose a time for this ceremony that seems appropriate for your family, and tell family members that you are planning to have a "Bubble Prayer." See the notes below for guidance.

2. Blow a stream of bubbles and ask these two questions:

*How do these bubbles move?* (They float. They fall to the ground. They hang in the air. They pop.)

*What do they look like?* (They are round. They have lots of colors. They are different sizes.)

3. Conclude the question time by saying, *"Bubbles are so special. They have lots of colors. They come in different sizes. They fall to the*

*ground. They pop. I love looking at bubbles, and sometimes I wish they didn't pop. Today we are remembering [name of person who died], and we have so many different things to think about. We are going to have a very special Bubble Prayer now."*

4. Instruct each person to blow a stream of bubbles and say, *"God, thank you for [person's name]."* Then watch as the bubbles fall to the ground and pop before the next person's turn.

5. At the end, everyone says, *"Amen."*

**Notes**

- Some families will choose to do this at the gravesite, on the day of a burial, or outside a church or funeral home on the day of a memorial service. An advantage to this time is the powerful connection it has to the strong emotions of that day. Also, choosing to do this ceremony at the gravesite on the day of a burial offers children a ceremony geared toward them, on a day that does not typically have child-friendly elements.

- Other families might choose to do this activity at a time that is somewhat distant from the memorial or graveside service. An advantage to choosing a later time is that the family has had some time to process the death, and the grief is not as fresh and new.

- This ceremony is listed as age 7+ because a child younger than 7 may not have an understanding of what has actually happened. Certainly younger children can appreciate bubbles, but they may not be able to participate fully in the understanding of what is happening, or the significance behind it. Follow your instincts or ask for help from a trusted minister, therapist, or friend.

*After a Death: Bubble Prayers*

---

- This is a very moving ceremony, one that is likely to cause adults to tear up. Use the tears as an opportunity to remind children that it's okay to be sad when someone dies or when we remember them. If someone is likely to cry uncontrollably or sob, it is wise to ask an additional family member, friend, or pastor to participate in the ceremony as well so there is someone to help the children feel protected and secure.

- If you choose to do this ceremony at a graveside or church where many people will be present, keep in mind that the sight of a family blowing bubbles might be misunderstood or confusing to others. Consider informing others ahead of time of your plan in order to make it a meaningful spiritual moment for your family.

**Variations**
- Instead of, "Thank you, God, for [name]," choose a different phrase. Some options:

  *"Goodbye, [name].*

  *"The death of one that belongs to [God] is precious in [God's] sight"* (Psalm 116:15, NCV).

  *"I thank God every time I remember [name]"* (Philippians 1:3, paraphrase).

- At the end, allow the children to blow bubbles and play (if appropriate).

# After the Death of a Pet

*St. Francis Service*

When I was an adult, my dad confessed to me that he was a little nervous about showing my childhood home to prospective buyers when we were moving. The reason, he said, was all of the crosses lined up in the garden in the backyard. The crosses were burial grounds for a variety of fish, hamsters, and other household pets that had passed away and been laid safely to rest in our backyard. He wondered if people would be reluctant to buy a house with an obvious graveyard in the back. Though the crosses might have looked a little unusual to the outside world, I look back on those childhood funerals with fondness, as they helped bring closure for me when my pets died. Children are naturally sensitive to life and death, and they often feel the death of pets very deeply. When a pet dies, it provides an opportunity for families to acknowledge the child's feelings and teach that all life is to be respected. This St. Francis service is short, and it teaches children about Francis of Assisi, an early Franciscan friar who is remembered for his love of animals.

Once, a mother of a special eight-year-old boy asked me to help her son cope with the death of his fish. It was his first experience with anything that had died. I used this activity, and I recommend it to all families in similar situations.

**Designed for Ages 4+**

**Materials**
1. Pet's body in a box to be buried (optional, and if appropriate)
2. Liturgy printed below
3. Special rock, either a nice rock from the yard or a decorative rock purchased from a craft store

*After the Death of a Pet: St. Francis Service*

---

**Time Investment:** 10–15 minutes
**How To**
1. Prepare for the service by digging a hole in the yard where the pet will be buried (optional).

2. Decide who will lead various parts of the liturgy below. Older children can do some of the reading or prayers. Take the time to write out each child's part on a separate piece of paper. The adult leading the liturgy can point to the person when it is his or her turn.

3. Gather everyone together for the liturgy below.

### St. Francis Service Liturgy
We have all gathered together to say goodbye to our [dog/cat/fish/etc.] named [pet's name]. All of God's creatures are important in the world. One man, St. Francis, also loved animals and taught us this prayer.

*Let's pray:*

*Lord, make me an instrument of your peace,*
*Where there is hatred, let me sow love;*
*Where there is injury, pardon;*
*Where there is doubt, faith;*
*Where there is despair, hope;*
*Where there is darkness, light;*
*Where there is sadness, joy.*

*Today we might be sad that we have lost our pet, [pet's name], but we are thankful for the opportunity to remember [him/her].*

*Let's hear a special reading about God's creatures:*

*"All Things Bright and Beautiful"*      *— by Cecil Alexander*

*All things bright and beautiful,*
*All creatures great and small,*
*All things wise and wonderful,*
*The Lord God made them all.*
*Each little flower that opens,*
*Each little bird that sings,*
*He made their glowing colors,*
*He made their tiny wings.*
*The purple-headed mountain,*
*The river running by,*
*The sunset, and the morning,*
*That brightens up the sky;*
*The cold wind in the winter,*
*The pleasant summer sun,*
*The ripe fruits in the garden,*
*He made them every one.*
*He gave us eyes to see them,*
*And lips that we might tell,*
*How great is God Almighty,*
*Who has made all things well.*

*Let's go around and each share one memory of [pet's name] that is special to us today. If you don't want to share anything, say, "I pass."*
(Each person takes a turn and shares a memory, if they choose.)

*After the Death of a Pet: St. Francis Service*

---

### Burial

If your family is choosing to bury the pet, this is the time that the family will place the pet in the ground and cover the pet with dirt. Say, *"Now we will cover [pet's name] with dirt as we prepare to leave [him/her] in the ground."* After the pet is buried, take the stone and place it over the grave and say, *"We will now set this stone over the place that [pet's name] is buried to remember [him/her] when we pass by."* If the pet will not be buried, just skip this element.

### Prayer

Someone says, *"Let us pray together now: God, we thank you for the many gifts you give us, including the gifts of the sun and the moon, the flowers and the trees, the birds of the air and the fish in the sea. We thank you for the life of our pet [name] and the good memories we have shared together. Let us be people like St. Francis of Assisi who love all of your creatures. May we be people of peace and compassion and love. Amen."*

### Benediction

Someone says, *"We will go from this place remembering that God created all living things and that God cares about each of us and all the creatures of the world. Amen."*

### Notes

- "Do dogs go to doggie heaven?" "What happens to my fish after it dies?" The Bible is silent on this topic, though some scholars are uncomfortable with talk about pets and animals in heaven. This liturgy doesn't reference where the pet is now. One appropriate answer is, *"It's a mystery what happens after we die, but we do know that God loves the world and everything in it."* I have left mention of heaven out of the liturgy because I don't think it's the most important emphasis.

- During the burial of the pet, if desired, allow each family member to take part in covering the pet with dirt to symbolically participate in this act of giving the pet up.

**Variations**
- For those who live in apartments or cannot bury the pet outside for whatever reason, place the stone somewhere in the house.

- Paint or decorate the rock ahead of time or after the service as a more permanent memorial.

- Instead of a stone, put a framed picture of the pet somewhere indoors.

# Anxiety

*Wash Away Worries*

Adults often look at the life of a child and think, "Children don't have a job, a marriage, or dependents to take care of. They have no responsibility. They play and have their needs met. Ah, the easy life." We are even quick to remind children, "Wait until you are in the real world, then you'll know how hard it really is!" The truth is, though, children do live in the real world—their world. And a child is faced with any number of anxieties on a daily basis. This ceremony allows children to express their worries in the presence and safety of a caring adult and then have a moment to ceremonially "wash them away" and call on the Holy Spirit to carry them.

**Designed for Ages 4+**

**Materials**
1. Chalk
2. Bucket with sponges, or a garden hose
3. Sidewalk or driveway (see variations for options for apartment/ condo dwellers)

**Time Investment:** 10–30 minutes

**How To**
1. When your child or teen comes to you with concern or worries, ask if he or she would like to do an exercise with you in which you "wash your worries away together." If the child says yes, grab your chalk and head outside!

2. Tell your child that you'll take some time to draw (or write) your worries out on the driveway together. It's important that the adult do this activity with the child so that the child doesn't feel singled out because of her worry. Tell your child that at the end she will

have the opportunity to explain her drawing or words, but that she doesn't have to if she doesn't want to.

3. At the end of the drawing time, ask your child to explain his drawing or worry if he would like. Model this by sharing some of your worries.

4. Together, fill a bucket with water and find sponges, or get out the garden hose.

5. Wash away your chalk drawings with the sponges or the garden hose. As you do, say, *"Holy Spirit, we give you our worries and fears. Take them away."*

6. Conclude with a hug and a prayer:

*"Holy Spirit, we have a lot of worry and anxiety. Help us to have peace and calm in our hearts. Amen."*

**Notes**

- I advise adults to share some, but not all, of their concerns to model to children how to be both public and private in their sharing of concerns. There are times when we want to share our worries with others, and there are times when we'd rather keep them private. Modeling that God hears all of our anxieties, even the unspoken ones, is a great relief for children.

- There is a strong temptation in this exercise for parents to either suggest solutions to these problems or to minimize the problems. Both of these instincts are born out of the desire to be genuinely helpful to the child. I encourage parents to resist the urge to do this. Perhaps during the activity you will think of some solutions you

*Anxiety: Wash Away Worries*

would like to present to your child at a different time. One way to approach this is to do the activity as written, then later say, *"You know, I was thinking about when we washed away our worries, and I had some ideas. Would you like to hear them?"* If the child says yes, offer your suggestions gently. If she says no, respect her desire to work through the problem herself. Certainly, there are exceptions to this, worries in which parents must get involved for the safety and protection of their children. However, consider doing the follow up after the washing away ceremony to allow the activity to stand alone as an exercise in quiet meditation.

• Adolescence is a time when worries abound! Don't be so quick to assume your teenager doesn't want to do an activity like this. During the teen years it is especially important to allow for symbolic drawings that might be worries "in code," and to not press your teen to divulge every detail to you. Follow up can happen in gentle ways as well: "I was wondering about that drawing from earlier. How's that all going?"

**Variations**
• Try this activity with personal chalkboards, a dry erase board, or even a pencil and eraser.

• Write down the worries and paint over them.

# Family Ceremony to Mark a Divorce

Divorce can be one of life's most stressful events—not only for the couple, but also for children. Though there is nothing that can take away the stress and grief of a divorce, having a ceremonial moment to mark the occasion and remember the presence of God is a powerful memorial that provides a sense of closure.

This script is written with the assumption that both parents will be present at the ceremony. Because of this, parents should resist the urge to go "off script" for this one. By design, this is a simple ceremony, and keeping to it as written will buffer against a tense moment or arguing.

This ceremony is not a forum for sharing feelings or asking questions, but rather for marking the moment and providing a structured way to remember it. Presumably, there will be other times when children's questions will be answered and feelings discussed. The ceremony should take place after the legal divorce has occurred, and parents should plan the ceremony together beforehand.

**Designed for Ages 7+**

**Time Investment**
10 minutes for the ceremony, plus preparation time before

**Materials**
1. A pin with a symbol on it for each member of the family; it doesn't matter what the symbol is, but it is important that the pins all be the same, as a reminder that even after divorce all members of the family are still connected. (Some examples are a heart, cross, dove, or Celtic knot.)
2. A candle and matches

## Family Ceremony to Mark a Divorce

---

3. A written script of the words that will be said and who will say them (use the guide below)

**How To**
In preparation, both spouses meet and talk through the ceremony. If spouses cannot agree on the form of the ceremony, or if the planning meeting does not go well, abandon this idea and seek counsel from a pastor or counselor about an alternate ceremony that might be meaningful. Decide who will take each of the parts below.

**Gathering**
At the agreed upon time, everyone gathers together.

**Opening Words**
*"Everyone is feeling different things on this day when we officially mark a new change for our family. Even though it is difficult, we gather together to remember that God is with us to light our path."*

**Lighting of the Candle**
Light the candle, saying, *"This candle represents the hope we have in good and dark times. Amen."*

**God's Promise**
*"God says, 'I know the plans I have for you, plans to prosper you and not to harm you, to give you hope and a future.' We know God loves and protects each member of our family and will be with us wherever we go."*[5]

**Presentation of Pins**
*"These pins are all the same. We have chosen a [describe the symbol] because [describe why it's important]. Though we will not all live*

*together as a family, we are all connected, and God loves each of us completely.*" Each member of the family puts a pin on another member of the family, making sure that each person has a chance to put a pin on for someone else and no family member is left out.

### Sending Peace

"*Our family has changed in big ways, [parent] and [parent] are no longer married, but we are still connected through you, our children. Even though our family has changed, we want you to remember that God's love for us never changes. God's love is like a circle that has no beginning and no end. Let's make a circle before we go.*" Everyone stands in a circle. Hold hands and say, "May we all know God's love today and every day. Let us go in peace."

### Notes

- You may want to plan for some quiet time after the ceremony, or for a trusted friend or family member to be with the children immediately afterward to give time and space for everyone to absorb the weight of the moment.

- Because of the stressful nature of divorce for all involved, some families might choose to ask for a trusted friend or spiritual advisor to help by being present at the ceremony. Make sure both parents agree on the person involved.

### Variations

- Ask a trusted mediator to conduct a service for you using the one above as a guide.

- Instead of a pin, use a piece of jewelry or other significant item.

# Traumatic Current Event

*Snuggled under God's Wings*

When I was an elementary student, the Challenger space shuttle exploded. In college, the Columbine Massacre happened. Then, soon after graduation, 9/11/2001. Each of these traumatic news stories affected me differently at different stages of my childhood, adolescence, and early adulthood. Though there are heartbreaking stories of violence and death in the news every day, there are some that seem to be too much for the soul to bear.

On December 14, 2012, I experienced my first traumatic news event as a mother. It was the day a 21-year-old man went on a shooting spree in a public elementary school, killing 26 people—20 of them children. On that day, and for many days afterward, the only thing I wanted to do was to be with my children and to hug and kiss them and to protect them.

This ceremony brings parents and children together at a time when a traumatic news story has affected the family. The beauty of this activity is that it gives children a space to talk about their feelings if they want to, but it does not demand that they speak at all. It also helps children to feel safe, protected, and sheltered.

*"[God] will cover you with [God's] feathers,*
*and under [God's] wings you can hide."* (Psalm 91:4a, NCV)

**Designed for Ages 6+**

**Materials**
1. Paper
2. Scissors
3. Pen/pencil/crayons
4. Faux feathers and glue (optional)

**Time Investment:** 10–30 minutes
(Depending on how elaborately you decorate your birds)

**How To**

1. Draw several large birds on writing or construction paper. Use the template provided here or create your own.

2. Invite children to the table for a special activity.

3. Say, *"Today you may have heard a little about [X event]."*

Describe the event that has happened in bare terms, using age-appropriate language. See the notes for guidance.

*Traumatic Current Event: Snuggled under God's Wings*

---

4. Say, *"I want you to know that you are safe and protected. Sometimes I want to snuggle you up like a [Mommy/Daddy] bird! There is a verse in the Bible that says:*

*[God] will cover you with [God's] feathers, and under [God's] wings you can hide"[Ps. 91:4a, NCV].*

*Today we can remember that God wants to snuggle and protect us just like your parents snuggle and protect you."*

5. Hand out the bird outlines and say, *"This is your bird to decorate. I have these materials (crayons, feathers and glue, markers, etc.) for you to use to decorate it."*

6. While each child is decorating a bird, talk a little about what has happened. (See notes for details.)

7. At the end of the activity, write the Bible verse under each bird and hang them up somewhere in the house as a reminder to the children that they are safe.

8. Give the children hugs and snuggles and say, *"You are like my baby birds and I will always do everything I can to make sure you are safe. I love you."*

**Notes**

- How you describe the event will depend on the children's ages and what they have already heard. A good guideline is to start out with less information and then encourage questions/elaboration from the children. Use your instincts about what is necessary to share, and err on the side of sharing less if you are unsure.

- During the discussion time, it is important to be truthful, but not volunteer extra information if it is not necessary. Be sure to reassure children that they are safe. Ask if the children have questions and encourage them to ask as many questions as they would like.

- While it is good for parents to be able to express emotion in their children's presence, ask for help from another adult (spouse, friend, etc.) if you don't feel you can remain calm and offer a sense of safety to the children during this activity.

- Children respond to these types of events in very different ways depending on age. Preschool children might mix up what is real and what is pretend. Pre-teens and teens might have much more complex and detailed understandings of the implications of traumatic events.

- If the event is catastrophic and likely to linger in the news for days or weeks, help children focus on good and positive things to do. See: "Compassion" and "Tolerance" in chapter 7 for two ideas.

**Variations**
- If there is a large difference in age in your children, do this activity one-on-one to allow for age-appropriate discussion, or involve teens in helping younger children with the activity. Have a follow-up discussion with the teens.

- For very young children, play "parent bird, baby bird." Drape a blanket over your arms, as your "wings" allow children to run and hide under them. Scoop them up and give them hugs. Let the children be the mama or daddy bird.

# After a Natural Disaster

*Butterfly Hug*

The butterfly hug is a calming technique created by therapist Luciana Artigas after Hurricane Pauline struck Mexico in 1997. It's a simple technique that can help children (and adults) relax and find peace. I learned about it when I was struggling to manage my own anxiety and panic attacks and have found it to be a useful tool for my children to find focus and rest. In researching this technique, I learned that Ms. Artigas developed this technique after one of the young children she was counseling asked, "Who will embrace me after you are gone?" Determined to come up with a way for children to feel accompanied in their trauma, Ms. Artigas and her husband developed the butterfly hug. The butterfly hug is a great reminder to children that there is nowhere we can go God is not with us. With practice, children can learn to practice the butterfly hug without the aid of a parent or guide.

**Designed for Ages 5+**

**Materials**
None

**Time Investment:** Varies

**How To**
1. Say, *"The psalmist says this about God, 'Suppose I had wings like the dawning day and flew across the ocean. Even then God's powerful arm would guide and protect me. Or suppose I said, "I'll hide in the dark until night comes to cover me over." But you see in the dark because daylight and dark are all the same to you.' [Psalm 139:9–12 CEV] This passage reminds us that God is always with us, in darkness and in light. Let's ask God to be near to us and to help us find calm and focus."* Guide your children through steps 2–8.

2. Sit or lie in a relaxed position.

3. Take a couple of deep breaths to begin to calm down and relax.

4. Cross your arms across your chest so that your fingertips rest just under your collar bone. Fingers should point more toward the top of the head, rather than the side of the body. Thumbs can interlock, or not, depending on what is most comfortable.

5. Gently close eyes, or softly focus ahead.

6. Alternate tapping fingers, left and right, at whatever speed feels most comfortable.

7. Continue to breathe deeply while tapping, left and right. Keep tapping for at least three minutes.

8. Either end the butterfly hug naturally (when the children feel calm and ready) or by saying *"Thank you, God, for peace. Help us to feel peace whenever we feel worried or unsafe."*

**Notes**

- Though this practice is listed as a ceremony for after a natural disaster, it can also be used as a spiritual practice for children who struggle with rest and worry. Remember that it takes patience and practice.

- Also, this practice works well with the Bedtime: Night Time Blessing in chapter 1. Practice the butterfly hug for a few minutes, and then say a blessing for children.

*After a Natural Disaster: Butterfly Hug*

---

**Variations**

- Take turns leading the Butterfly Hug.

- Sing a song and tap the wings of the butterfly in tune with the song. Singing is a great way to control breath and reduce stress.

# Marking a Pregnancy Loss

*Make a Memory Box*

This practice is one that was suggested to me by readers after the first release of this book. Pregnancy loss is so common, yet so seldom discussed in our society. Parents should not hesitate to reach out for help with this practice from trusted ministers or spiritual leaders for the support they need during this difficult time.

**Designed for All Ages**

**Materials**

1. Beautiful box

2 Large ribbon to tie around the box

3. Memories to add to the box; some ideas:

- Ultrasound pictures

- Baby hat, blanket, or clothes

- Handmade drawings, poems, or paintings about the baby

- Small toys

- Condolence cards from family or friends

- Pregnancy journal or other memories from pregnancy

**Time Investment:** 30 Minutes

*Marking a Pregnancy Loss: Make a Memory Box*

---

**How To**

1. Have family members help in gathering materials together for the memory box.

2. Explain to everyone that this box is a special way to remember the baby's life and his/her importance in the family.

3. Talk about the items one by one together as you put them in the box.

4. If children have made drawings to include, allow them a chance to talk about them and what they mean.

5. Before the box is tied up with the ribbon, explain that it can be opened again when the family wants to remember the baby.

6. Tie the ribbon around the box and place it in a prominent location somewhere in the home.

**Notes**

- This practice assumes that there has been some age-appropriate discussion already about the loss before making the memory box. Experts advise being direct and answering children's questions with simple and brief answers, not being afraid to show sadness or other emotions, and being honest and clear.

- Talking about heaven and angels to young children is a natural parental instinct, but it can be confusing for young children who are very literal. A simple thing to say is something along the lines of, *"We are sad that the baby is not with us, but we know that God is taking good care of him/her and we don't need to worry."*

- Reassure children that the loss is not their fault.

- This is a practice that a family minister, pastor, or good friend might be willing to assist with in order to also minister to grieving parents.

**Variations**
- Your family might choose to put the box in a less prominent location for a time, depending on what feels natural and appropriate in your situation.

- Plant a special tree or plant in your yard or church in memory of the baby. Put a photo of it in the box.

# Separating from Family after a Visit

*Remembering Good Times*

One of the hardest things about being far away from grandparents is saying goodbye after a visit. This practice emphasizes God's presence with us no matter where we are and creates a lovely memory for grandparents and children alike.

**Designed for All Ages**

**Materials**
1. Flying Wish Paper (see www.traci-smith.com/resources for recommended sources)
2. Pens / writing utensils

**Time Investment:** 10 minutes

**How To**
1. On the day you are parting (or the evening before) gather together (preferably outside, for safety) and think about some of the lovely times you have shared together during your visit.

2. Write down some of your memories on the wish paper.

3. Light the paper and watch it go up to the sky. Mention that though the paper is gone, the memories remain in your minds and hearts.

4. As your wish goes up to the sky, say this prayer: *"God, we thank you for the wonderful time we had together and pray that you will watch over us when we are apart. Amen."*

**Notes**
• Be sure to have the proper fire safety equipment around in case the wish paper lights something else on fire. This is not common, in my

experience, but be prepared!

- This is one of few practices in the book that requires special materials. If you don't have Flying Wish Paper, never fear! Do one of the variations below.

**Variations**
- Write the memories on paper and either rip it up and throw it like confetti, or burn it and watch the ashes form.

- Draw pictures instead of writing words; this is especially useful for younger children.

# Part Three

## Spiritual Practices

# Chapter 5

*The Spiritual Practice of Prayer*

# Photo Prayers

It's hard to pray with a very young child or infant. This photo prayer is a way to engage babies and toddlers who are learning to connect people and faces. It also sets up a routine for praying for others that can develop into more advanced prayers.

**Designed for Babies and Younger Toddlers**

**Materials**
Photos of important family members and pets

**Time Investment:** 1–5 minutes, plus 10–30 minute preparation

**How To**
1. Print photos of family members and other significant people in the family's life. Choose photos in which faces are large and prominent.

2. Place the photos near a chair where you can sit just before bedtime.

***For the Practice***
1. After the child is dressed and ready for bed, sit with the photos and hold the child on your lap. Show the child each picture and say, *"God Bless [name]"* (*"God Bless Grandma," "God Bless Angie," "God Bless Papa," etc.*).

2. As the child's age and speaking ability develops, have the child point to the photo, repeat the name, or say the blessing with you.

3. After the final picture say, *"Amen."*

**Notes**

- This exercise is effective in its simplicity. Over time, even a very young child notices the routine of sitting down, looking at the photos, and saying the names. Resist the temptation to say more than the simple blessing.

- Keep the exercise sacred by looking at this particular set of photos only at prayer time.

**Variations**

- Instead of sitting in a chair with printed photos, walk around the house and touch photos that are hanging in frames or displayed on tables. As you walk by each photo, touch it and say, "God Bless [name]." The final destination is the child's bed, and you can end by placing the child in bed, saying a blessing (see chapter 1), and adding *"Amen."*

- Add other drawings or pictures and use phrases such as "God Bless The World" or "God Bless all the animals in the land and the fish in the sea."

- Add another sacred element, such as a special blanket or shawl to cover the child only during this prayer time, or turning on a battery-operated candle before you sit down.

# Matchbox Prayers

*God's Mailbox*

There is a simple activity from my childhood Sunday school class that I continued to remember for years afterward. The activity was to put a Bible verse in a decorated matchbox to keep as a reminder that God's word is always with us. The activity made a profound impact on me, in part, because the action of hiding a piece of paper in a tiny box felt like hiding away a secret. It had a very ceremonial feel to it. This activity allows children to explore the idea of telling their most profound thoughts to God, and hiding them away in a special box.

**Designed for Ages 6+**

**Materials**
1. Empty matchboxes
2. Construction or scrapbook paper
3. Glue
4. Scissors

**Time Investment**
20 minutes to make the box, plus 30 minutes for the activity

**How To**
Explain to the children that you are going to make a very special box, but do not reveal the box's purpose at first.

1. Cut a strip of paper that will wrap around the matchbox to cover it.

2. Glue the paper in place over the matchbox.

3. Cut small pieces of paper that, when folded, will fit inside the matchbox.

---

### Explain and Use the Prayer Box

1. After everyone has had a chance to make a box and cut the pieces of paper, explain the purpose of the box. The box is a prayer box. Family members can write their very special prayers on their pieces of paper, fold them up, and put them in their matchboxes. Explain, *"We can put our prayers in our boxes knowing that God hears each of our prayers, even if God doesn't always respond in ways we would have wanted."*

2. Help children find special places to put their boxes, and encourage them to take out old prayers and put new prayers in when they have special prayer requests to God.

### Notes

- Reassure children that their boxes are private, between them and God, and that you do not need to know everything they put in their prayer boxes.

- Use this activity to answer the children's questions about prayer as they come up. *"Why is it hard to know if God heard my prayer?"* or, *"I prayed for grandpa to get well and he still died! Did God ignore my prayer?"* Answer honestly and don't be afraid to say, *"That is a mystery."*

- Model the use of the boxes by having your own and talking about it.

### Variations

- Use another type of box instead of a matchbox.

- Decide which prayers you would like to write down as a family rather than having it be an individual project.

# Prayer Beads

When I worked as a Director of Youth Ministries, I always had Play-Doh, Silly Putty, and a variety of other trinkets on my desk and shelves. When students came in to my office to chat with me, they would sit in the chair, pick up a toy, and make conversation. As they settled in the chair, they would begin to talk. If the topic on their mind was heavy or difficult to discuss, they would fiddle with the toy, and it served as a way to help them focus. Often the toy was a way to get them to sit down and begin to talk. This variation on prayer beads is designed with this concept in mind. The string of beads is something for a child to hold on to and fiddle with when praying. Unlike a Rosary or other type of prayer beads, the beads do not have specific symbolism, nor is there a required number of beads. If there are prayer beads in your tradition, this practice can be modified.

**Designed for Ages 6+**

**Materials**
1. Glass beads of different shapes, sizes, and colors
2. Yarn, cord, or thread for stringing

**Time Investment:** 10–30 minutes

**How To**
1. Find a time when your family will not be rushed and can dedicate at least 10 minutes to this activity.

2. Give each member of the family an equal length of string or yarn and say, *"We're going to make prayer beads today. We will talk about how to use them later, but for now choose the beads you like the most and string them together on the cord. Choose beads that are special to you."*

3. As family members are stringing the beads, ask them the very open-ended question, *"How do you think these beads can help you to pray?"* There may be silence, but you may also find that you get a variety of unexpected answers about how the children intend to use the beads to help with prayer.

4. Suggest to family members that one way to use the beads is to have them in their hands while they pray to help them focus. See if anyone has other suggestions for how to use the beads to help with prayer.

5. When the beads are strung, secure the cord on both ends so the beads do not fall off, and put them in a special place for when the children will want to use them.

**Notes**
- If children are older and/or curious about other prayer traditions, use the time to explain how others use beads in their prayer traditions. Ask the children if there is anything about those traditions that appeals to them, and why.

- Children who enjoy crafts and colors can make prayer beads to give away as gifts as well.

**Variations**
- Ask children to assign meaning to each of three beads. (One bead to pray for family, one bead to remember to pray for the world, and one to remember to pray for self.)

- Ask children to choose a number of beads that has special meaning for him or her.

# Prayer Basket

In many churches and faith communities around the world, people bring their prayer requests to God via baskets or boxes or offering plates. Little slips of paper with people's deepest needs and requests are placed lovingly into these different vessels with the confidence and hope that they will be read and the requests lifted up to God. Why not have a family prayer basket with the same function? Those who visit your family can also be invited to contribute their requests as well.

**Designed for Ages 3+**

**Materials**
1. Small basket
2. Slips of paper
3. Pencils, pens, or crayons

**Time Investment:** Varies

**How To**
1. Place a basket in a prominent location in your home with slips of paper and pens or pencils beside it.

2. Label the basket "Prayers" or "We Pray for Each Other."

3. Leave the basket without comment for a while. As children and others ask about it, you can say, *"This is our prayer basket for now, or from now on if we like it. Anytime someone has a need they would like other people to pray for, they will write it down or draw a picture of it. Anytime someone wants to pray for others, they can go over to the basket, read what is inside, and pray about it."*

4. Clear the basket out periodically.

**Notes**

- It is very important to check the basket regularly. Be sure to designate an adult or responsible older child to check the basket regularly in case there is an urgent request that a family member would like to make using these means.

- The prayer basket need not be a permanent fixture in your home. Try having it available for a season or defined period of time.

- Invite family members to leave the prayer slips in the basket so everyone has the opportunity to read the requests.

- In my ministry as a pastor, it's always hard for me to throw away written requests. I prefer to burn them and to imagine that the requests are going back up to God one last time. While this is an optional practice, I advise against tossing the old prayer requests in the trash. The symbolism there, especially for sensitive children, is too much to bear. Recycling them, saving them, or burning them are alternatives.

**Variations**

- Instead of blank pieces of paper, make a fill-in-the-blank card that can be duplicated. The card might say, *"Today I am thankful for_____"* or, *"Today I would like to pray for_____."* Include a space for the person making the request to sign it.

- Younger children can draw pictures of the things they would like others to pray for.

- Decorate the basket as a family.

# Wind Prayers for the World

Many cultures and countries have the custom of hanging flags in the wind. The image is a reminder that as the wind blows, the prayers are carried away with it and everyone who is touched by the wind benefits from the prayers. Flags are left up, even when they are weathered and worn, and, then, eventually burned. In this prayer, the family makes their own prayer flags together and hangs them outside. For Christians, a prayer flag is a way to talk about the presence of the Holy Spirit. Evidence of the Holy Spirit's work is all around us, even if we can't see it at times. (See also "Pentecost" in chapter 2.)

### Designed for Ages 6+

### Materials
1. 5 x 10 inch squares of fabric
2. Hot glue gun or fabric glue
3. Yarn
4. Fabric markers, or fabric paint and paint brushes

**Time Investment:** 30–60 minutes

### How To
1. Explain the prayer flags, saying, *"This prayer is special, because we will write or draw it on our prayer flag and hang it outside. Then, when we look at our prayer flags outside, we will see them moving in the wind and remember how the Holy Spirit always hears our prayers. We can imagine that our prayers for the world will be spread around the whole earth, just like the wind."*

2. Ask each family member to answer the question, *"What is one thing that you hope for our world?"*

3. Give each family member a fabric square and fabric markers (or paint) and say, *"Let's draw a picture of what our prayers would look like or write a word to represent our prayer."*

It is easiest to orient the rectangles vertically. When the flags are completed, the top two inches will be folded over the string to hang, making a five inch by eight inch rectangle. Instruct family members to allow this room at the top for the flags to be folded over.

4. After designs are complete and dry, hang the flags. Cut a piece of yarn long enough to hold all of the flags with 2–3 inches of room between each. Fold the top of each flag over the yarn and secure it with hot glue or fabric glue.

5. Find a place outside to hang your flags.

**Notes**
• Fabric that is not sewn or finished in some way around the edges will fray easily in the wind. This is part of the evidence that the wind has moved through them!

• Doing an Internet search of prayer flags will yield rich galleries and examples from around the world for inspiration.

**Variations**
• Make flags out of construction paper or canvas.

• Make one large prayer flag that all the family members decorate.

• Hang the flags without decorating them, and guide family members in allowing them to represent whatever prayers are on their hearts and minds that particular day.

# Prayer Walk

When I ask adults in my congregation when they feel the presence of God most clearly, I often hear things such as "while hiking," or "when the sun sets," or "in nature." So often when we consider the wonders of God, we see evidence of God's creative power in snowfall, or rain, or wind. This prayer practice involves walking in nature and noticing the marvels of God's creation.

**Designed for Ages 5+**

**Materials**
(All of these materials are optional)

1. Paper bag, basket, or other container for collecting interesting things
2. Magnifying glass
3. Binoculars
4. Camera
5. Sketch pad and pencil or crayons
6. Any materials that you need on a hike (sunscreen, bug spray, sunglasses, lunch, etc.)

**Time Investment:** 30 minutes—2 hours or more

**How To**
1. Pick a day and location appropriate for a walk or hike outside.

2. Prepare for your walk and take with you items that are relevant for your context and weather conditions.

3. Introduce the idea of a prayer walk to your family by saying, *"We are going to go for a walk now to think about all of the special ways that we can see the work of God in the world around us."*

4. Choose a way your family might decide to identify how you see God on your walk. Some options:

a. Collect items along the way that seem meaningful and put them in a bag or basket (if appropriate; many parks and nature reserves don't allow the removal of any living things, so only take things such as leaves already lying on the ground, etc.).
b. Encourage everyone to take photos of places where there is evidence of God's work.
c. Draw sketches.
d. Write poems.

5. After the walk, gather together to share what you have learned by sharing your photos, drawings, and/or paintings.

**Notes**
- Consider doing this prayer walk, not only on a sunny or pleasant day, but also on days that are rainy, "too hot," "too cold," or otherwise not ideal. These imperfect days offer a rich opportunity to see evidence of God's work in ways that might not be apparent on other days.

- This activity will vary greatly depending on the interests and activities of family members. Consider allowing each family member to pick out the ways that he or she sees God's work. One person might photograph, while another collects things, and yet another sketches.

*Prayer Walk*

---

**Variations**

• Do this prayer walk inside at a unique location: a mall, church, etc. Take the same walk and travel the same route over a period of time (one time per month for a year, for example), and compare how observations change over time.

• Travel to a special location for the purpose of this practice. Try different national parks, or local parks and trails.

# Candle Prayers

In my first years as a minister, I was often overwhelmed with the privilege and responsibility of praying for other people. I shared my feelings with a spiritual director and said, "I worry I am forgetting someone who is counting on me to pray for them!" She nodded sympathetically and then taught me this simple practice. "Light a candle," she said, "and as it burns, you can watch the light radiate and the small bit of smoke rise up, and you will know that all of your prayers, the spoken and unspoken ones, go up to God." I never forgot that advice, and candle prayers are an important part of my own faith journey. This spiritual practice is very simple, and easy to explain to a child.

**Designed for Ages 8+**

**Materials**
Candle and matches, or battery-operated candle

**Time Investment:** 30 seconds—2 minutes

**How To**
1. Parent and child (or the whole family) gather in a dim or dark room and light a candle.

2. Say, *"This candle burning is our prayer. Just as the light fills up the dark room, we know that our prayers are lifted up to God. Let's sit here for a minute and watch the candle and know that our prayers are known by God, even if we don't know what we want to say or how to say it."*

*Candle Prayers*

---

3. At the end of a minute or so say, *"Now we are going to end our candle prayer. I will blow out the candle and we will all say 'Amen.' We will know that God heard our prayer."*

**Notes**

- Use battery-operated candles for homes in which little ones or pets are likely to run around and bump into them.

- This practice can easily be combined with the practice of the sacred meal, in chapter 6.

**Variations**

- Instead of blowing the candle out, let it burn in some visible part of the house for many hours. Remind the family that it is a visible sign of God's presence.

- Make the candle prayer specific. When someone has a special need, say, *"Let's light a candle and know that God hears our prayers.*

- *Tonight we light a candle for [name]."*

# Smartphone Prayers

When I was in the beginning stages of promoting the first edition of this book, I had the opportunity to present the ideas in the book at the *Faith Forward* conference, an annual conference for imaginative and creative children's and youth ministry leaders. If you ever have the chance to attend, I highly recommend it. At that conference I learned a version of this very special prayer from Lilly Lewin, who calls herself a curator of "free range worship." The thing I love most about this practice is how it uses the smartphone as a tool to bring focus to the prayer rather than seeing it as a distraction. I often hear parents ask, *"How can I get my teen off of his/her phone?"* This practice teaches how to use technology in service of spiritual practice rather than against it.

**Designed for Ages 10+**

**Materials**
Smartphone with at least 15 minutes of battery life remaining (preferably one smartphone per participant)

**Time Investment:**
5–10 minutes

**How To**
1. For this practice, one family member will act as the leader, and others will be participants. Rotate who serves as the leader in order to give everyone a chance to participate in the prayer.

2. The leader will call everyone together and explain the Smartphone Prayer. Say, *"This prayer moves through five different activities on our smartphones. Each is one minute long. I will tell you what to do*

*Smartphone Prayers*

---

*for each activity and then start my timer. When the timer rings, look up at me and listen for the next mission."*

3. Go through the five missions as follows, making sure the leader sets his/her timer after each instruction and calls everyone back together before presenting the next mission:

- Minute One: *Go to your text messages and take a look at the last five people in the recent messages, whether they are people you text regularly or people you don't know at all. Take this minute to pray for each of the five people listed there.*

- Minute Two: *Go to a news app or website and take a minute to scroll through the headlines. Pray for what jumps out at you as a prayer need this day.*

- Minute Three: *Go to the notepad and spend this minute typing out whatever comes to mind: praise, gratitude, confession, or requests to God.*

- Minute Four: *Go to your favorite social media site and spend this minute praying for the people who come up on your feed during this minute.*

- Minute Five: *Go to your photos. Take this moment to scroll through the most recent twenty or so photos. What prayers come to mind? Lift them up to God now.*

4. Follow up: After the five-minute prayer is over, take a couple of minutes to talk about the activity together using one or more of the following questions:

- *Was there anything surprising or unusual that you heard from God when you were using your cell phone to pray today?*

- *What was the most important prayer that came through today?*

- *How can we incorporate this attitude of prayer as we use our smartphones throughout the week?*

- *In your opinion, does technology draw us closer to God or farther away? Talk a little about your opinion.*

**Notes**
- Though this practice aims to use technology as a tool for fostering and encouraging spiritual practice, I still strongly encourage the practice of turning off or unplugging from electronic devices. The Lenten fasting from technology practice in chapter 2 is appropriate for use year round. All of the practices in *Faithful Families* can be enhanced by putting technology away while the practices are enjoyed. Certain practices are particularly suited for putting technology away.

- For more fantastic and creative prayer and spiritual practice, visit Lilly Lewin on the web at www.freerangeworship.com.

- For other ways to use smartphones to build community through a prayer service for youth groups or families who are far away from one another, visit www.traci-smith.com/resources.

**Variations**
- This practice is well suited to become an "add on" practice to other practices in *Faithful Families* or a part of a daily family or individual

*Smartphone Prayers*

routine. Try running through the Smartphone Prayer for five minutes before dinner, and then putting phones away for the remainder of dinner. For another variation, start the day with the prayer as a reminder to not let the phone dictate the day.

• Instead of using one phone per person, use one phone per family.

• Add different elements to the prayer that incorporate other often used apps on your smartphone.

# Chapter 6

## *Ancient Spiritual Practices*

# The Ignatian Examen

The Ignatian Examen is a way of praying that has been practiced for centuries. Ignatius, one of the early church patriarchs, proposed the Examen as a way of reflecting on one's day and growing closer to God. This variation is modified for families as an activity that can be done in the car or at dinnertime. Instead of being done individually in silence, it is done out loud.

**Designed for Ages 5+**

**Materials:** None

**Time Investment:** 5–15 minutes

**How To**

1. Each family member takes turns answering the following three questions:

*What are a few memorable things that happened today?*

*When was the time when you saw or felt close to God today, or saw God at work today?*

*When was the time when you felt farthest from God today, or felt that you missed an opportunity to share God's love?*

2. Questions are handled one at a time. As each family member shares, the other family members listen without comment or interruption.

**Notes**

- If a child responds with a shrug or, "I don't know," try a gentle prompt. "Anything that might have happened at school, or band practice?"

- If, after prompting, a child still says, "No," participation in the family Examen time should not be forced. Families might choose to require that all members stay present at the table and listen respectfully, but those who do not wish to share aloud can be encouraged to think about their answers in silence.

- This exercise differs from other family discussions or reflection times in that it is not a "back and forth" type of conversation. Family members do not offer commentary or follow-up questions. Follow up can happen away from the table, if necessary.

**Variations**

- Alternate who shares on which days.

- Some families may enjoy doing this practice every day, others might pick a specific day of the week to it, or to include it as a part of the sacred meal (described in this chapter).

- Allow family members to hear the questions one at a time and reflect on their own answers silently, or in a journal, rather than sharing them with the rest of the family.

# Lectio Divina (Divine Reading)

For centuries, Christians have read the Bible using Lectio Divina. Lectio Divina is a practice of reading a text several times and letting the meaning sink deep into the heart of the listener. It is not a study of the text in the traditional sense, but rather a form of meditation using sacred text as its starting point.

This practice involves four steps: lectio (read), meditatio (meditate), oratio (pray) and contemplatio (contemplate). Each step has a slightly different focus. Some have compared Lectio Divina to eating—in which the food is tasted, savored, digested, and then becomes a part of the body. Lectio Divina can be used with any sacred text that is significant to your family.

**Designed for Ages 9+**

**Materials**
Sacred text for reflection

**Time Investment:** 15–30 minutes

**How To**
*Before Beginning*
The leader of the practice should review the suggested texts and find one that will be appropriate for the family. Consider everyone's age, the complexity of the text, and the length of the passage. Part of the mystery of Lectio Divina is how passages that seem straightforward at first reveal new layers of meaning when they are read and meditated upon. Don't shy away from passages that seem too simple. Conversely, do not fear difficult passages. Sometimes things leap out of obtuse passages in unexpected ways.

### For the practice of Lectio Divina

1. Choose a time for your family to give the Lectio Divina practice a try. Some Ideas: at a meal, first thing in the morning, just before bed.

2. The leader says, *"Today we have the opportunity to hear a passage in a new way. We will read through it four times. Four of us will read it out loud. Each time through we will focus on something different. The first time through we will focus on lectio, which means 'read.' Listen carefully for what this story is about."*

3. One person reads though the text slowly and carefully. After reading it, the reader asks *"What would you say, in one sentence, this text is about? Don't worry if your answer is different from my answer or other's answers; it's just what you are thinking and feeling."*

4. After everyone has had a chance to answer if they wish, the leader gives the text to the next person and says, *"Now we will continue with meditatio, which means 'reflect,' and [name of person] will read the passage for us a second time, slowly and carefully. As [he/she] reads, we'll wonder what the text means."*

5. After the second reading, the leader says, *"We already talked about what this text is about; what do you think it means?"*

6. Allow all to offer their thoughts on the meaning of the text, and then say, *"Now we will move on to the third part, oratio, which means 'prayer.' [Name] will read the text this time, and as [he/she] does, we will think about how we feel when we hear this text."*

## Lectio Divina (Divine Reading)

7. After the third reading, the leader asks all to explain how they felt when they heard the text. When everyone who wishes to speak has spoken, the leader says, *"Now we will move on to the last step, which is contemplatio, which means 'contemplate.' We will listen for what we want to do when we hear this text. [Name] will read it for us one last time."*

8. After the final reading, everyone discusses what the text asks the reader to do.

9. When everyone has had a chance to respond to the fourth and final question, the leader closes by saying, *"We have had a chance to really think about this text and wonder about what it says, what it means, how we feel when we read it, and what we want to do because of it. It is so exciting that each of us can hear different things as we hear the texts together. Amen!"*

**Notes**

- The leader should guide family members in such a way that each person's comments stand alone. That is, when one person offers thoughts or feelings, others shouldn't add to them, question them, or dispute them, but should simply listen and wait for their turns to share. In this way Lectio Divina is a sharing, rather than a discussion, much like the practice of the Ignatian Examen. Each thought is valid.

- Practice makes perfect! I recommend families try Lectio Divina a few times before deciding if it's a good practice for their family.

**Variations**

- Instead of vocalizing the answers to each question, ask each participant to write or draw answers, and then share all reflections at the end.

- Allow this to be a reflective process through journaling or silence rather than an out loud practice.

- Work through one section of a text over several weeks, or even the whole year.

# Bodily Prayers

Christianity is rich with traditions that involve the body: from pilgrimages to chants to the sign of the cross, the body is used in different ways. Yet, for most children, "Fold your hands and bow your head," is the only instruction given with regard to a prayer posture. There are many prayer positions seen in the Bible and elsewhere: kneeling, lying flat on the ground, lying with one's forehead to the ground, praying with hands to the sky. Children are naturally drawn to a variety of different postures and are often quite receptive to experimenting with their bodies in prayer. This activity is playful, and it allows children to experiment with different ways of talking to God.

**Designed for Ages 2–8**

**Materials:** None

**Time Investment:** 5 minutes

**How To**

1. Tell children, *"Sometimes when we pray, we are quiet with our heads bowed and our fingers clasped, but, sometimes, we can pray while we move around. We can reach to the sky or curl in a tiny ball or kneel or lay flat on the ground."*

2. Say, *"Let's practice it! Who has a prayer?"*

3. Ask children for a short (one sentence) prayer. (Example: "I pray grandma is better," or, "Thank you, God, for this day.")

4. Take the suggestions and practice praying in a variety of postures: first "traditionally," then reaching up to the sky, then curled in a tiny ball, then lying flat on the ground.

5. Ask, *"Which did you like the best?"* and, *"Which did you like the least?"*

6. Repeat with each person's prayers.

**Notes**
- Be prepared with a few prayer suggestions in case a child doesn't have one.

- Allow children to laugh and smile and be silly during these moving prayers. God loves and accepts them for who they are as children, and prayer isn't always a solemn occasion.

**Variations**
- Instead of going through all of the postures for each prayer, pick one of the postures and try everyone's prayer in that way, changing the posture each day. (For example, use the traditional way on Monday, reaching to the sky on Tuesday, etc.)

- Allow children to make up their own prayer postures (for example, skipping, standing on one leg, etc.).

- Invite children to invent prayer postures for a familiar prayer such as the Lord's Prayer.

# The Labyrinth

Labyrinths are maze-like structures that have their roots in ancient mythology. Christians have used them for centuries as a way to center themselves, look inward, and meditate. In English we often use the words "labyrinth" and "maze" interchangeably. The significant difference between a maze and labyrinth, however, is that a maze has multiple and confusing routes with many dead ends, whereas a labyrinth has only one path to follow the whole way through. Part of the experience of walking a labyrinth is trusting in this truth. Though the traveller can't see the end, he has to trust that he won't get lost. In this version of the spiritual practice, family members make their own finger labyrinths on paper plates and use them for meditation and reflection.

**Designed for Ages 6+**

Materials
1. Paper plates with a flat surface area and raised edge
2. Pencils
3. Puffy paint
4. Labyrinth template

**Time Investment**
To make the labyrinth: 10 minutes plus drying time; to do the labyrinth practice itself: 1 to 10+ minutes, depending on the child's age and attention span

**How To**
*Each Person Makes a Labyrinth*
In pencil, draw the outline of the labyrinth on the paper plate. Use the example on the next page as a guide.

1. Trace over the pencil outline with puffy paint, using either a continuous long line or dots. Be sure to use a fairly thick layer of paint so there will be a raised edge.

2. Allow the paint to dry overnight or longer.

### Practice the Labyrinth

1. Explain that the idea of the labyrinth is to journey to the center and then out again as slowly and meditatively as possible. There is nothing specific to think about. Try to be open to the experience.

2. Demonstrate how to use your finger to move along the raised path. The labyrinth journey can be taken with eyes open or eyes closed.

*The Labyrinth*

---

3. Set apart some time for each person to take a journey to the center of the labyrinth and back out again. Remember to emphasize that the journey is to be taken slowly. Challenge children to move their fingers as slowly as they can without stopping.

4. After the experience, come back together and talk for a brief time about the experience. Ask:

- *Was it hard or easy to go slowly?*

- *What did you think about the experience?*

- *Would you like to do it again sometime?*

**Note**
- Some families will want to journey through their labyrinths at the same time, and in the same room, while others will prefer to send each person to their own place in the home for the practice. Experiment with both options and decide which is better for your family.

**Variations**
- If this activity is well received in your family, try packing the finger labyrinths with you on a vacation so you can journey through them in a special location, or take a special trip with the labyrinth journey in mind.

- Use the website www.labyrinthlocator.com to find a walkable labyrinth to travel together.

- Try this with black paper plates and glow-in-the-dark puffy paint, and use it at night or in the dark.

**Morning Songs**
"You Are My Sunshine"
"This Is the Day"
"Rise and Shine"
"All Things Bright and Beautiful"
"This Little Light of Mine"
"Morning Has Broken"

**Evening Songs**
"Kumbaya"
"God Is So Good"
"Twinkle, Twinkle, Little Star"
"Silent Night"
"Brahms Lullaby"
"All the Pretty Little Horses"

4. **Read**
Psalm 145

*I will exalt you, my God and King,*
*and praise your name forever and ever.*
*I will praise you every day;*
*yes, I will praise you forever.*
*Great is the LORD! [God] is most worthy of praise!*
*No one can measure his greatness.*

*Let each generation tell its children of your mighty acts;*
*let them proclaim your power.*
*I will meditate on your majestic, glorious splendor*
*and your wonderful miracles.*

*The Daily Office: Morning and Evening Prayers*

---

*Your awe-inspiring deeds will be on every tongue;*
*I will proclaim your greatness.*
*Everyone will share the story of your wonderful goodness;*
*they will sing with joy about your righteousness.*

*The LORD is merciful and compassionate,*
*slow to get angry and filled with unfailing love.*
*The LORD is good to everyone.*
*[God] showers compassion on all of [God's] creation.*
*All of your works will thank you, LORD,*
*and your faithful followers will praise you.*
*They will speak of the glory of your kingdom;*
*they will give examples of your power.*
*They will tell about your mighty deeds*
*and about the majesty and glory of your reign.*
*For your kingdom is an everlasting kingdom.*
*You rule throughout all generations.*

*The LORD always keeps his promises;*
*God is gracious in all God does.*
*The LORD helps the fallen*
*and lifts those bent beneath their loads.*
*The eyes of all look to you in hope;*
*you give them their food as they need it.*
*When you open your hand,*
*you satisfy the hunger and thirst of every living thing.*
*The LORD is righteous in everything he does;*
*he is filled with kindness.*
*The LORD is close to all who call on him,*
*yes, to all who call on him in truth.*
*[God] grants the desires of those who fear him;*

*[God] hears their cries for help and rescues them.
The LORD protects all those who love him,
but he destroys the wicked.*

*I will praise the LORD,
and may everyone on earth bless his holy name
forever and ever. (NLT)*[6]

### 5. Reflect
For the morning practice, someone says, *"Take some time to reflect quietly about the day before you. What kind of day would you like to have today? Are you nervous or excited about anything coming up today?"* For the evening practice, someone says, *"How was your day today? How did you see God at work today?"*

### 6. Share
Each person has the opportunity to share one thing about the day to come or past if he or she chooses, but are not required to.

### 7. Benediction
*Morning:* Say, *"Let us go out into our day now, ready for the joys and challenges ahead."*
*Evening:* Say, *"As we go now to sleep, may we remember God's faithfulness not only this day, but all our days as well."*

Everyone says, *"Amen,"* and goes about their day, or to sleep.

### Notes
This practice should be modified to best fit the ages of children in your family. Those with small children will want to shorten the talking time and perhaps increase the singing to two or three songs.

*The Daily Office: Morning and Evening Prayers*

---

- Some older children and adolescents who might not want to sing with the family might be encouraged to bring a favorite piece of music for the family to listen to together.

- Remember, part of the beauty of this practice is the rhythm it creates for daily life. Therefore, aim to try the practice for at least a week. What doesn't go well the first day might seem easy by the end of the week. After doing the practice regularly, check in with the family:

  *"How is it going? How can we change our Morning/Evening Prayer? What have we learned?"*

**Variations**
- Take turns deciding who will lead Morning and Evening Prayer. The leader gets to choose the song, do the reading, and say the benediction.

- Substitute the songs/readings with your family favorites.

- Vary or alter the words for one or more parts of the liturgy. Use on-line or printed resources (or your own creativity) to help you write alternate liturgies.

- Commit to doing Morning and Evening Prayer for a specific length of time (a month, the season of Lent, two weeks, etc.)

- Commit to doing Morning and Evening Prayer when you are on vacation.

# Chapter 7

## *Other Spiritual Practices*

# Silence

*Listening Car Rides*

Silence. Sweet, sweet silence. Many parents long for the elusive silence. Oh, to experience freedom from noisy games, chatter, and bickering! Silence, more than just a time to enjoy the absence of chaos, is a powerful tool for connecting with God. So often we speak of prayer as a time to talk to God, but if prayer is truly a conversation, we must make time to listen, too. This practice takes advantage of car rides.

In the Introduction, I spoke a bit about the need for spiritual practices to never be punitive. This is particularly important for this practice. The goal is for children, over time, to associate quiet with a sense of listening to God and peace. If parents enter in to "Listening Car Rides" in a flurry of anger, saying, "I said QUIET!" children may associate quiet with tension or punishment and come to resent it. If it is treated as something mysterious and spiritual, children may come to appreciate and embrace it.

**Designed for Ages 5+**
(Length of time should be adjusted according to age)

**Materials:** None

**Time Investment:** Varies

**How To**
1. Choose to do a Listening Car Ride at a time when the family is not rushing out the door. Allow an extra five minutes to explain the activity and dawdle on the way to the car. It is important for everyone to be in a peaceful state of mind before beginning.

2. Before leaving, gather everyone together and explain in a very quiet voice, almost a whisper: *"This is a Listening Car Ride. That means we are going to listen to hear if God has anything to say to us in the silence of our car ride. We won't talk to anyone in the car—unless there is an emergency—from the time I say 'Amen' until we get to our destination and I say 'Amen' again."*

3. When everyone is settled in the car, say, *"Now we will try our Listening Car Ride. We will be silent to see if God has something to say to us. We might not hear anything, and that's okay; it's important for us to be 100 percent silent and quiet from the time I say 'Amen.' Ready? Here we go."* Then pray, *"God, we thank you for this quiet car ride. Help us to listen closely to you while we are in the car. Amen."*

4. Drive to your destination in silence. When you arrive, say, *"God, thank you for allowing us the opportunity to listen for your voice. Amen."*

### Notes

- Start very slowly with this one; a 1–3 minute car ride is more than enough time for the first ride. Praise children for their good work on this. It's hard to be quiet! Gradually increase the time of silence and listening. Remember, this activity will be more challenging for some children than others.

- When children test this activity by speaking, making noise, etc., gently get everyone on track by saying, *"Remember...quiet listening time, please!"* If the activity unravels, abandon it for another time. (See "What should I do when something goes wrong?" in the "Frequently Asked Questions" section.)

*Silence: Listening Car Rides*

---

**Variations**

- Instead of total silence, try this with quiet (and wordless) music playing.

- Add a time of discussion afterward:

- *"How did you feel about listening time? Did you hear God say anything to you?"*

- For children who enjoy silence and listening, consider adding a journal that they can use to write or draw what they have heard God say during this time.

- Try this activity at home with a timer rather than in the car.

# Imagination

*Star Pictures*

Imagination and faith go hand in hand. The Bible says, "Faith is the assurance of things hoped for, the conviction of things not seen."[7] As we cultivate a life of faith, we must rely on our imaginations. We envision a better world and we imagine what God is like. We must be imaginative to see things from another's perspective. Most children are gifted imaginers; we as adults need only to tune in to what is already there. This activity allows families to imagine together, and it uses stars as a starting place.

**Designed for All Ages**

**Materials**
All of these materials, except for the starry sky, are optional and will vary depending on your location and season.

1. Starry night sky (see note)
2. Blankets or sheets
3. Refreshments (hot chocolate, lemonade, etc.)
4. Bug spray
5. Flashlights

**Time Investment:** 15 minutes to an hour or more

**How To**
1. On a clear, comfortable night with a lot of stars visible, gather everyone together for a nighttime imagination star party.

2. Start the activity by saying, *"There is a verse in the Bible that says, '[God] determines the number of stars / and calls them each by name.'*[8] *Isn't it amazing to think about how all of these stars were created by God? God must be so big and creative to put all of these stars in the sky."*

*Imagination: Star Pictures*

___

3. Lie down on blankets under the stars and invite everyone to look at the stars and talk about what pictures they can find in the stars.

4. After a time of finding star pictures, close with a prayer:

*"God who created the stars in the sky, thank you for giving us time to use our imaginations to see pictures in the sky. Bless us and help us to have a good night. Amen."*

**Notes**

• This activity is closely tied to one's environment. For those who live in urban areas where light pollution makes it difficult (or impossible) to see stars, try the first variation below.

• Nonverbal toddlers and babies can sit outside and enjoy the night air for this activity, even if they can't yet participate in the star finding activity.

**Variations**

• For some, this activity must wait until vacation or a time when there are stars visible in a location other than home. If this is too rare an occurrence in your family, you can recreate your own starry sky with a little preparation. Find an extra-large piece of black butcher paper and randomly place white dots on it with white paint. Don't worry about putting them in any pattern—put some close together and some spread out. Hang the paper from the ceiling in a room and lie on the floor under low light. Do the activity as described under your "starry sky."

- Try this same activity with clouds. Use this Bible verse to begin:

  *"Whenever I bring clouds over the earth and the rainbow appears in the clouds, I will remember my covenant between me and you and all living creatures of every kind."* You can say, *"Even though there is no rainbow in the sky, we still see lots of clouds. God made the clouds and the sky and everything in it."* [9]

# Waiting

*Water, Air, and Sky*

Waiting is hard, for children and adults alike. Sometimes we wait for small things like the bus or our turn in line. Sometimes we are waiting for something that happens slowly and gradually, almost imperceptibly, like water evaporating from a glass. Throughout life we must wait. We wait for healing or for our dreams to become reality; we even wait to understand our faith. This activity is a visual reminder that many of the things we hope for in life come slowly.

**Designed for Ages 8+**

**Materials**
1. Pitcher with 8 ounces of water
2. Empty glass

**Time Investment:** 5 minutes of active time, up to a month or more of waiting

**How To**
1. Someone reads aloud Romans 8:25, which says, *"If we hope for what we do not yet have, we wait for it patiently"* (NIV). The reader asks two questions:

*(1) "What does it feel like to wait a long time for something?"* and *(2) "What is something you are waiting for now?"*

2. After the questions, say, *"We are going to start an activity now about waiting, and it will take a very long time. Each of us is going to pour a little bit of this water into this glass, and then we will put the glass somewhere we can check on it every day. We will wait to see how long the water stays in the glass and how long it takes to evaporate. As we pass by and see how long it is taking, we might feel*

*discouraged or wonder if it is ever going to happen, but slowly, very slowly, all of the water will evaporate. The water becomes part of the air, but it is such a slow process we hardly notice it."*

3. Take turns pouring the water into the glass, and decide where to put it in your house. Choose a place where people will pass by it regularly but will not disturb it.

4. Walk by the glass on a regular basis and take note of how the water is evaporating. Comment with family members on the progress from time to time. When the water has finally evaporated completely, schedule a time the family will come back together for a discussion.

5. Read the Bible verse together again:

*"If we hope for what we do not yet have, we wait for it patiently."*

Ask: (1) *"How did it feel to wait for the water to evaporate?"* Give prompts if nobody comes up with a reaction. *"Was it boring? Did you feel like it was happening so slowly you could hardly see it? Was it exciting to imagine that the day would finally be here?"* and (2) *"What are some things that we wait for that take a very long time?"* Some ideas for this question include healing, a new baby, perfecting a skill, etc.

6. Close with a prayer:

*"Thank you, God, for this lesson about waiting. Help us to remember that you are with us, even when waiting for something important that takes a long time. Amen."*

*Waiting: Water, Air, and Sky*

---

**Notes**

- It takes a very long time for 8 ounces of water to evaporate from a glass. Though there are variables that change the amount of time it will take, you can plan on anywhere from two weeks to a month, on average. Although many things affect the rate of evaporation, two main things will accelerate or slow down the process: (1) the surface area—the wider the glass, the quicker evaporation will happen; (2) the temperature—the colder the ambient temperature, the slower the evaporation.

- Some children will be drawn to this activity and check on the water daily, or even more frequently, to see its progress. Others might be tempted to ignore it. The empty glass might remain empty for a long time before some remember the activity at all. When someone finally notices, call everyone together for the discussion questions.

**Variations**

- Color the water with food coloring to make it even more noticeable (and less likely the water will be thrown away!).

- Label the glass "the waiting glass," or something similar.

- Try syncing the water evaporation with a key event in your family's life. See which happens first, the evaporation of all the water or the event you are waiting for (birth of a new baby, for example).

# Meditation

*Make Quiet Time Bags*

Now more than ever, it's important for children and adults to take time for inner peace and meditation. This time can be used to listen to God, clear one's mind, and let go of the day's worries and cares. Often with meditation, we think of sitting still and silent. Since this doesn't work for many children, everyday activities can bring opportunities to meditate on hearing God's voice. When done intentionally, even something like putting together a puzzle is a chance to quiet oneself and listen for God's voice. In this exercise, each family member makes a "quiet time bag" to be used for personal meditation. Later, the family spends time together, each person working on the activities he or she has chosen. In this way, the family is encouraged to take some time to unplug, quiet themselves, and be still.

**Designed for ages 3+**

**Materials**
1. A special bag for each member of the family
2. Materials that each family member enjoys, and which contribute to his or her sense of inner peace, quiet, and calm. This will vary for each family member depending on personal interests and age. Some examples: knitting or crochet, an inspiring book (with either words or pictures), art supplies, a simple quiet game (nothing with an on/off switch!), blocks, etc.

**Time Investment**
30 minutes to prepare the bags, 15 minutes—1 hour for quiet time

**How To:**
*Prepare the Quiet Time Bags*
1. Explain to family members that, from time to time, your family will be observing quiet time. During this time, each family member

*Meditation: Make Quiet Time Bags*

---

will be engaged in the activities found in the quiet time bag. During quiet time it will not be permitted to watch TV or use any other electronics.

2. Hand out bags to older children and allow them to select their own activities for their bags. Provide guidance and suggestions for what might go in the bags. Assemble bags with (or for) very young children.

3. Store the bags until it is time to use them.

**For Quiet Time**

1. Choose a time for the practice. Enforce an electronics-free rule and quiet ambiance.

2. Distribute the quiet time bags to each family member and allow each person to go his or her own way for the time allotted.

3. Gather together at the end of quiet time to collect the bags and talk about the experience. *What did you do? Did you enjoy your quiet time? Was it easy or hard to enjoy your rest?*

**Notes**

• Once bags are assembled, families can experiment with different lengths of quiet time or different quiet time routines.

• Part of the appeal of quiet time is its novelty. Help family members put something in the bags that will only be used at quiet time so that quiet time becomes something to look forward to.

**Variations**

- Instead of assembling one's own bag, have one family member assemble them for the rest of the family as a surprise. Alternate who makes the bags and experiment with each family member's suggestions.

- Create one bag the whole family grabs from.

# Compassion

*Secret Helpers Week*

Awareness is central to compassion. Those with the ability to be compassionate are often very tuned in to the needs of others. Like other skills, compassion can be learned and practiced. This simple family practice helps children not only recognize ways in which they can show compassion to other members of the family, but also allows them to experience acts of kindness and reflect on how good it feels when someone helps them.

**Designed for Ages 5+**

**Materials:** None

**Time Investment:** 30 second—2 minute intervals throughout a week, plus a 30 minute sharing time at the end of the week

**How To**

1. Explain to the family that for the period of one week, effective immediately, the family will be having a "Secret Helpers" week. Anytime someone sees a family member with a special need, he or she will make the special effort to go help that person, immediately, without being asked, and without expecting something in return. Because it is secret helpers week, no family members will draw attention to what they are doing.

2. Throughout the week, parents and caregivers will vocalize little clues that help children remember the challenge for the week. "Wow, Daddy helped me carry the groceries in from the car; he's really paying attention to secret helpers week," or, "I can't wait to do something special for each of you tomorrow for secret helpers week."

3. At the end of the week, have a conversation about the experience. Use the following questions as a guide:

- *How did it feel to give special help to your family members this week?*

- *Were there times that you did something special that your family members noticed? What about times that they didn't notice?*

- *What things did others do for you this week?*

- *Was it easy or hard to help family members?*

- *Should we do this again? How often?*

**Notes**

- One of the limitations of this exercise is that it seems to imply that family members are only helping others out because of this special exercise. During the debriefing session, a parent can point this out by saying, *"It's nice to help each other out all the time, not just during the secret helpers week."*

- Some children might benefit from a little (or a lot) of prompting and encouragement: *"Wow, it looks like Dad could use someone to hold that dustpan for him; maybe you would like it to be one of your jobs for secret helpers week!"* or, *"Your sister has had a hard day at school, why don't you and I pick a flower from the garden and leave it in her room with a note? It will be a chance to participate in secret helpers week."*

*Compassion: Secret Helpers Week*

---

**Variations**

- Try secret helpers days rather than weeks to get the family used to the idea.

- At the beginning of the week, have each family member draw a name of someone else in the family and have each person focus on helping the person whose name they drew. At the end of the week, try to guess who your helper was.

- Do this activity on a regular basis (every Monday, every 5th of the month, every March, etc.)

# Hospitality

*Serving an Honored Guest*

In college, I had the opportunity to live together with a group of students in an intentional community. We shared our meals together and were mentored by a pair of wise house parents who taught us things we were not learning in our academic classes. Our house mom had a knack for making guests feel welcome. Everyone that came by felt loved and cared for. One evening someone asked her, "How do you entertain so well? Where did you learn it?" I will never forget her response. "I don't entertain," she said. "Entertaining is all about making the host look good. I try to be hospitable. Hospitality is about the guest." The distinction between entertaining and hospitality is a good one to teach young children. Hospitality is a spiritual practice designed to make guests feel welcome and loved while they are in your home. This practice makes it fun to serve an honored guest. The preparation is just as important as the event.

**Designed for Ages 6+**

**Materials**
Varied depending on the preferences of your guest

**Time Investment:** 30–60 minutes preparation, plus visiting time

### How To
1. Take turns inviting an honored guest to your home either for a meal, snack, or family outing.

2. Before the guest arrives, one family member takes special care to find out some information about the guest. What is her favorite food? Favorite dessert? Favorite drink? Does the guest have any allergies, or is he on a special diet? What is your guest's favorite color? Does she like flowers or balloons?

*Hospitality: Serving an Honored Guest*

3. The family member who has found out the information about the honored guest shares it with the family and together the family makes a plan for how to make the guest feel welcome and loved. Can we serve the guest's favorite foods on plates in her favorite color? What would he like to do? The focus is on the guest's preferences, not the hosts'.

4. Invite the guest over and shower him or her with love and hospitality.

5. After the guest leaves, reflect on the visit. How did the guest feel? How did the family do as the hosts?

**Notes**

- One of the more challenging aspects of hospitality is being hospitable to someone who is, in some way, difficult to invite into your home. In the Bible, Jesus talks about inviting people who are outcasts and making them into honored guests. Encourage children to treat everyone who comes into your home as an honored guest.

- Be sure to remind children that good hospitality doesn't have to be expensive or fancy. It is also okay to have little touches that are not unique to your guest's preferences. Every single detail need not be a personal favorite of the guest.

- Choose guests for this activity who know your family well and have visited before. You might want to describe the activity to your guest ahead of time so he or she doesn't feel overwhelmed or put on the spot by the intentionality of the exercise.

**Variations**

• Have a "hospitality month" when honored guests are invited through-out the month.

• Incorporate hospitality into the practice of the sacred meal. (See chapter 6.)

• Invite several guests to one meal or dessert and discuss how the preferences of all the guests will be juggled and accommodated.

# Waiting

*Paper Chains*

When my boys wait for trips to Grandma and Grandpa's house, it's often hard for them to visualize or for us to effectively explain how long it will be until we get there, particularly since periods of time such as "in two weeks" have little relevance for their little minds. We started to make a paper chain to keep track of the days, and it's become a sweet and meaningful practice for our family.

**Designed for Ages 2–6**

Materials
1. Strips of paper to make "links" in a chain (as many pieces of paper as there are days)

2. Tape or stapler

**Time Investment**
About five minutes to make the paper links and then one minute per day to make the chain.

**How To**
1. Tell children that when the paper chain is complete, the event for which you are waiting will be complete. ("When there are no more papers to make a chain, it will be time to go to Grandma and Grandpa's house!" or, "We're moving on the day our paper chain is complete.")

2. Each day, take turns attaching one link to the chain and noticing how it grows. As you do, reflect on waiting and patience with one of the following optional questions:

> • *In Galatians 5:22–23a [NRSV], patience is described as a "fruit*

*of the spirit," along with love, joy, peace, kindness, generosity, faithfulness, gentleness, and self-control. Why do you think it's so important to have patience?*

- *Is it easy or hard to wait for something? Why?*

- *Our chain is growing every day. What are some other things that grow? What makes things grow?*

**Notes**
- This practice is listed for children ages 2–6 because of its simplicity and ease of use. Use one of the variations below, or the other waiting exercise in this chapter (Water, Air, and Sky), for older children.

- This practice can become a tradition as you wait for the same thing, year after year (birthdays or holidays, for example.)

**Variations**
- Make the chain first and take one link off each day.

- Write something on each link about the event your family is waiting for. Read all of the thoughts after the chain is made.

- Advent is a great time for this practice, as waiting and Advent go together so well. Look for the printable Advent calendar in my Etsy shop (https://www.etsy.com/shop/AuthorTraciSmith) and enter the code 3989072 for 50 percent off the calendar!

# Surprise

*Planting Surprises*

One of my readers once told me about a mother who asked her children every day to tell her something that surprised them on that day. I love that! To be able to look at one's day with surprise and delight is a wonderful way to go through life. This practice encourages surprise in two ways. First, surprising things are noticed and recorded, and, second, there is a surprise as the seeded paper is planted and later turns into flowers.

**Designed for Ages 7+**

**Materials**
1. Seeded paper (see notes for sources)

2. Markers

3. Basket

4. A place to plant the seeded paper (either a pot with dirt or an area in the yard with nice soil)

5. Trowels or shovels

**Time Investment**
10 minutes to set up, plus 1 minute per day to record surprises; 20 minutes for planting ceremony

**How To**

**Collect the Surprises**
1. Cut the seed paper into shapes or strips.

2. Place the strips next to a basket and markers and place in a prominent place in your home.

3. Instruct each family member to write a way each day that God has surprised him or her, and place the paper in the basket.

**Plant the Surprises and Watch them Grow**

1. When the strips of paper have all been written on, find a time to have a planting ceremony.

2. Gather everyone together around the pot with dirt or the area outside. Say, *"We've been collecting our surprises for some time on these strips of paper. Let's read them and remember the ways that God has been surprising us."*

3. Read through the surprises one at a time. Ask family members to elaborate on them if they wish.

4. Say, *"There is one more surprise left! The papers we've been using for our surprises will turn into flowers when we plant them! Let's plant them and see our surprises grow."*

5. Plant the surprises in the ground or pot, using the instructions that came with the seed paper, and watch as they turn to wildflowers in time.

**Notes**
- This activity will, undoubtedly, fail some of the time, in that the seed paper will not sprout 100 percent of the time. If this happens, it would be a great opportunity to talk about the mysteries of nature.

*Surprise: Planting Surprises*

---

Explain that sometimes things sprout up without much effort on our part, and sometimes the opposite is true.

- Visit www.traci-smith.com/resources for a current list of places to find the plantable seed paper, or check:

- www.botanicalpaperworks.com

- https://www.etsy.com/shop/Davita

**Variations**

- Do just the first part of the activity, writing on regular paper, and collect the surprises, forgoing the special paper and planting surprise.

- Have small children draw pictures of surprising things instead of writing.

- Have a regular time (before bed, at dinnertime, or first thing in the morning) to record the surprises as a family.

# Tolerance

*The Golden Rule*

Readers of the first version of this book have often talked to me about how much they value tolerance and respect for other religions. When I lead workshops, I'm often asked, *"How can we raise children who are conscious of other religions and their traditions?"* Usually, my answer is that people should make sure you get to know friends of other religions and learn what is important to them. Living in a religiously diverse community is a blessing in this regard. The following simple activity is another way to get the conversation going.

**Designed for Ages 5+**

**Materials**

1. Pieces of paper with the words of Luke 6:31 written on them (Luke 6:31 says, "Do to others as you would have them do to you," in the NIV translation, but you can use whatever version of the Bible you'd like.)

2. Art supplies to decorate the page, such as crayons, markers, glitter pens, stickers, or colored pencils

3. Poster depicting the golden rule in various religions (see www.traci-smith.com/resources for links to sources)

**Time Investment:** 15–20 minutes

**How To**

1. Gather everyone together to talk about the golden rule. Say, *"One of the most important things that Jesus said was that we should do to others as we would have them do to us. Some people call this 'the golden rule.' What does 'the golden rule' mean to you?"*

*Tolerance: The Golden Rule*

2. Pass out the coloring sheets and art supplies and have everyone decorate them as you continue your conversation.

3. Say, *"One interesting thing about 'the golden rule' is that many different religious teachers have said similar things."*

4. Show the poster or printout of the golden rule in other religious traditions and read a few of them.

5. Discuss the golden rule with one or more or of the following questions:

- *What do you think it means that so many of the world's religions have variations of 'the golden rule'?*

- *Do you know anyone who is a member of another religion? What do you know about his/her religion? Would you like to talk with that person about the golden rule?*

- *Why is it important to follow 'the golden rule' no matter what?*

**Notes**
- The depth of the discussion your family is able to have will depend largely on children's ages and exposure to interfaith discussion. This activity is a great one to pull out again every few years and see how ideas have changed and grown.

- Different faith traditions and denominations have different ways of talking about other religions in relationship to one's own. If you have questions about how to approach this topic with your family in a manner consistent with your faith tradition, consider talking with a leader in your place of worship. When in doubt, err on the side of tolerance, love, and respect.

**Variations**

- Consider inviting a friend of another religion over for a special meal. (See "Hospitality" in chapter 7.)

- Skip the coloring part and just do the discussion. Conversely, do the coloring part and skip the discussion. Or, do the whole practice over two days.

- Post the golden rule poster in a prominent place in your house and refer to it often.

# Beauty

*Focus on God's Beautiful Creation*

With our societal addiction to cell phones and other electronic screens, sometimes I wonder if we miss out on really absorbing the beauty of nature all around us. We're so eager to capture and share everything around us. We take pictures and videos, but do we really let beauty sink deep into our souls and leave a permanent impression there? This practice encourages deep observation of nature and creation of mental pictures of the world around us that use all five senses.

**Designed for Ages 4+**

**Materials**
None

**Time Investment:** 5–15 minutes

**How To**
1. Go outside and find something beautiful to focus on: a sunset, a flower, a beautiful sky, or anything else interesting.

2. Instruct everyone to notice all of the details they can about the beautiful thing and talk about them together. Ask questions such as: *"How does it look? Are there any sounds associated with it? If you can touch it, how does it feel? Does it have a smell?"* Take a good look at this thing, more than you might normally, and notice details you might not have noticed before.

3. After some time of observing together, go back inside and try to recreate the memory again. Instruct everyone to close their eyes. Ask questions such as: *"Can you still picture the same scene? What do you remember? What was the most beautiful part, in your mind?"*

**Notes**

- This practice is fantastic for vacation or other special times when it's tempting to rush through the "to do" list without pausing to notice the beauty all around.

- Similarly, when visiting an art museum or other attraction, use this practice to help make lasting memories of the visit.

**Variations**

- After coming inside, try to recreate the scene by drawing or painting it.

- Do the "three snapshots" activity: At the beginning of an important day, instruct everyone to plan to take three mental snapshots of special or beautiful moments in the day. At the end of the day, ask each person to recall his or her snapshots and share with others.

# Epilogue

I remember one evening a while ago when my then two year old was playing with a large stuffed giraffe. At one point he declared it was time for the giraffe to go "night-night," and so he lovingly laid the giraffe down on its side, put his hand on its head, said a gibberish "blessing" and concluded with an enthusiastic "Amen!" Though my child didn't yet know the words for God or Spirit, and though he has not yet had the opportunity to wrestle with some of the more difficult questions about life, he was beginning to practice faith. Like a child who plays with a toy kitchen, my son was experimenting with faith when he laid his giraffe down to sleep. My heart was filled to overflowing when I saw how something so simple had taken root in his heart and mind.

I know that readers of this book will see great things happen when you engage these traditions, ceremonies, and spiritual practices in your homes. I commend you for your desire to impart the gifts of spirituality, imagination, and faith into the hearts and minds of your children. I encourage you to contact me via my website at http://www.traci-smith.com and share your stories of how your family used the ideas in this book. May the God of Peace bless you and your family.

Amen.

# Supplemental Material

# Guide For Grandparents

When I'm presenting workshops about faith practices and children, grandparents attend with almost the same (if not more) frequency as parents. I hear them say things such as:

*"I am the person who is present to pass on faith to my grandchildren; I want them to grow in faith and I need some ideas."*

*"My children don't go to church, but they don't seem opposed to the idea that I would share faith with the grandchildren."*

*"I want to share my faith with my grandchildren, but I'm worried about crossing a boundary or interfering somehow."*

If this describes you, here are some tips and suggestions I think will help as you go through some of the traditions in this book:

- **Be the initiator (or guardian) of tradition for your family.** Grandparents and tradition go together like peanut butter and jelly! So many among us remember how every year grandma and grandpa would *(fill in the blank)*. Create a tradition with your grandchildren that you stick to as much as you possibly can. Perhaps your tradition is to take the grandchildren to church on particular holidays or to say a special prayer with them before every meal. Use any of the traditions in this book, or others you have designed. Whatever tradition you choose, make it your own. Traditions should be memorable, they should be simple, and they should happen frequently.

- **Make faith connections with your grandchildren about the things you already do with them.** Do you go out and look at stars with your grandchildren at night? Take the opportunity to talk to them about how God made the stars and the world and everything in it. Do you have bird feeders outside? Let your grandchildren fill them up and talk to them about how important it is to take care of God's creatures. Do you cook or bake with your grandchildren? Make extra goodies and have your grandchildren help you take them to folks who need them, explaining that you do this because you believe it's important to care for others. Your grandchildren will get the message, I promise. It's not necessary to have a separate "faith time" with your grandchildren, just weave it into what you are already doing!

- **Provide faith connections with your grandchildren during key transition moments in their lives.** In this book, I call these "ceremonies," but you can call them rituals, or celebrations, or whatever you like! Find a way to "mark the moment" with your grandchildren in a way that honors faith. Perhaps it is the first day of school and you'd like to honor that moment with a remembrance that God is with your grandchildren wherever they go. The same is true of graduation, or the birth of a new grandchild. Ceremonies can also be valuable with your grandchildren when they experience hard times. Be there for them when they are anxious, lose a pet, or have to deal with the hard current-events stories they are sometimes faced with.

- **Think creatively about spiritual practices you can teach your grandchildren.** Often when we think about spiritual practices to practice with our grandchildren, we remember prayers and meals or bedtime. This is great, but there are so many other spiritual practices we can use, too. Again, if you're not interested in coming up with your own, you can use the ones I lay out in in this book. Some examples are: creative prayer, imagination, and meditation. There are also plenty of ancient spiritual practices that speak to

*Guide For Grandparents*

---

children today. Things such as the daily *examen*, the labyrinth and *lectio divina* can all be used with your grandchildren.

A lot of times people ask me some variation of this question: *"I raised my children in the faith, but they don't go anymore. How can I get them to take the grandchildren to church?"*

This is a tough one, and certainly something that I hear a lot. Each family situation is unique, but I have a few "dos and don'ts" that grandparents I've talked to have found to be helpful:

**DON'T** say things that inspire guilt or drive a wedge between your children and you.

**DO** talk with your children respectfully and with genuine curiosity about why they're not interested in church. Perhaps you will find that there is something about the theology in which your children were raised that doesn't seem to fit with what they believe now. Many children who were raised in the '70s, '80s and '90s found that, when they became adults, the faith of their parents was too judgmental, too exclusive, too difficult to relate to. They need sympathetic ears who will listen to the kind of faith they are looking to embrace. There are plenty of faith communities out there that are daring to reimagine faith and Christianity, but a lot of people don't know where to look, or how to start.

**DO** share your faith in ways that are natural and not preachy. One of Francis of Assisi's most famous quotes is, this: "Preach the gospel at all times. If necessary, use words." Your grandchildren and children will continue to remember how important your faith is to you when they see how it affects the way you life your life. When I learned how to crochet, my brother said, *"I remember how grandma used to crochet those little hats for babies in the hospital. I always thought that was really cool."* I never knew she did that, but clearly it had a profound impact on my brother.

**DO** ask your adult children how they feel about your incorporating your faith stories or activities with your grandchildren. If you say, *"I would love to make a bird feeder with the children and talk to them about how God cares for the earth; is that okay?"* your children are likely to say, *"Yes! That sounds great!"*

**DON'T** tell your grandchildren everybody must believe the same way you do. One of the number one reasons I hear from parents of young children of why those have decided to stay away from the church is that they feel the church is too closed-minded and is not open to a diversity of opinions. Even if you have strong beliefs about right and wrong, your children and grandchildren may not. It will help you to maintain a strong relationship with your family if you are clear that you are only sharing your own beliefs and do not expect them to think exactly the same way you do.

**DO** provide unconditional love and acceptance of your children and grandchildren, no matter what.

For more resources on sharing faith with grandchildren, visit www.traci-smith.com/resources.

# Guide For Ministers and Ministry Leaders

When *Faithful Families* was first released (under the title *Seamless Faith*), many children's ministry leaders, pastors, youth pastors, and other children's ministry professionals shared how they used the book to help families deepen their faith at home throughout the week. I've compiled some of their ideas here and added some extra tips for those of you who are religious professionals to make the most out of this book with your congregations or communities.

- **Give the book as a gift** to families at back-to-school time, on the occasion of a baptism, at Christmas, or any other time your congregation finds it appropriate. We've added a special presentation page in the front of the book you can use for this purpose to make the book a special keepsake for years to come.

- **Use *Faithful Families* as the basis for a book study for parents during an adult Sunday school class or evening study.**

- **Excerpt practices from *Faithful Families* in your church's newsletter and refer back to the book.** Feel free to excerpt up to six practices from *Faithful Families* for use in your church's newsletter or publication. Practices must be excerpted exactly as written and not altered or changed in any way. Please include the following language in the article: "This practice excerpted from the book *Faithful Families: Simple Practices for Daily Family Life* by Traci Smith. Published by Chalice Press, 2017. All rights reserved. Used by permission."

- **Offer to be present or lead some of the practices in the book that are especially conducive to guided support.** All of the practices in *Faithful Families* are designed to be led by families on their own. Even so, there are particular practices that can be led by a minister or ministry leader to help families through a tough time.

The practices in chapter 4, Ceremonies for Difficult Times, are particularly conducive to pastoral support.

- **Model a practice during a children's moment, Sunday school class, or special event with children.** Use the instructions as they are written in the practice, and then end by telling children that they can continue their practice at home with their families. Practices that are particularly conducive to this type of instruction are all of the prayers in chapter 5, The Spiritual Practice of Prayer, as well as the activities in chapter 7, Other Spiritual Practices.

- **Lead a 90-minute workshop using the principles in the book.** *Faithful Families* lends itself to a special event in which parents gather together and learn about the practices in the book. Some churches have had parents gather together for a workshop while children have their own special time together. Others have made *Faithful Families* a focus of an adult Sunday school hour or two-week series. Use the Special Event Guide to help you plan an event like this.

# Special Event Guide

Use this guide to create a special 90-minute event to present the practices found in *Faithful Families* to your congregation, parents' group or school group. Tailor the event to suit your individual community needs. Many have used this template to create meaningful events in their congregation. I would love to hear how your event goes! Get in touch at http://www.traci-smith.com or on Facebook at www.facebook.com/TraciMarieSmithAuthor. Blessings on your event!

**GOAL:** Create a training event from start to finish for parents that will help them incorporate faith practices into their families' lives. Participants will have a time to interact with other parents; learn about traditions, ceremonies, and spiritual practices; and come away with practical ideas that they can use at home.

**OVERVIEW:**
This event is intended to be 90 minutes long. A suggested timeline is as follows:

1. Gathering: Introduction / snacks / welcome (about 15 minutes)

2. Presentation: Teaching simple traditions, ceremonies, and spiritual practices (about 30 minutes)

3. Roundtable discussion (about 20 minutes)

4. Question and answer time and a presentation of other resources (about 25 minutes)

Before beginning, gather a team to work through the logistics of the event. Smaller congregations may not require a team. Logistics to consider:

*Special Event Guide*

---

- Where and when will the event be held?

- What will the event be called?

- How can we get the word out?

- How will we make it possible for children to come with their families? What will they be doing while the parents are learning?

- What are the logistics specific to our community?

  **1. Gathering (about 15 minutes)**
  In most church traditions I know, a gathering time is essential, to grab some coffee or treats and mingle. Some things to consider for your gathering time:

  - Help everyone feel welcome by using name tags or introductions

  - Introduce the topic clearly without intimidating

  - Balance different family styles/makeup

  - Introduce the topic

  - Set a friendly and easygoing tone

  **2. Presentation (about 30 Minutes):** The 30-minute presentation is the part of this event that requires the most preparation by the leader or minister, but using the guide below makes it very easy to prepare. Some will find it useful to prepare a handout using the outline as a guide for parents to fill in and take notes as they listen.

Be sure to practice the presentation to check the timing.

A. *Introduce the Presentation* by talking about how important it is to incorporate traditions, ceremonies, and spiritual practices in all aspects of daily family life. Explain traditions, spiritual practices, and ceremonies one at a time using their definitions in the introduction. For each, give three examples of each using the ideas from the book or your own ideas before moving on to the next.

B. *Introduce Traditions*

1. What is the definition of a faith tradition, according to the book?

2. Give three examples of faith traditions:

- Choose a tradition for every day (chapter 1).

- Choose a tradition for holiday / holy day (chapter 2).

- Choose a third tradition of your choice (for either every day or a holiday).

C. *Introduce Ceremonies*

1. What is the definition of a faith ceremony, according to the book?

2. Give three examples of faith ceremonies:

- Choose a ceremony to mark a life transition (chapter 3).

- Choose a ceremony for a difficult time (chapter 4).

- Choose a third ceremony (for either a life transition or difficult time).

D. *Introduce Spiritual Practices*

1. What is the definition of a spiritual practice, according to the book?

2. Give four examples of spiritual practices:

- Choose a prayer (chapter 5).

- Choose an ancient spiritual practice (chapter 6).

- Choose an "other" spiritual practice (chapter 7).

- Choose a fourth spiritual practice (that is either a prayer, spiritual practice, or other).

E. *Conclude the Presentation* by reminding the participants that they will next have a few minutes to discuss the presentation with the people at their table and look at the material in depth. (This is also a good time in the flow of the event to take a short break and reconvene.)

**3. Roundtable discussion (about 20 minutes):**
Give participants time to discuss the material in the presentation and talk with each other about challenges of implementing some of the suggestions. If, as a part of the event, everyone has a copy of the book, allow participants time to browse and discern which practices

might work well for their family. Whether or not everyone has a copy of the book, the discussion is valuable. Use the following questions as a guide, but be sure to choose questions you think will work best for your context and community.

- *What traditions, ceremonies, or spiritual practices (if any) were a part of your childhood growing up?*

- *Which of the practices presented today (or in the book) seem to be a good practice for your family? How will you adapt or modify it to make it work for your family?*

- *What is the hardest part about passing faith on to children or practicing faith at home?*

- *What questions do you have about using this material or implementing these practices?*

**4. Question and answer and presentation of other resources (about 25 minutes):** Conclude by allowing some time for participants to ask questions. For help, refer to the FAQ section of *Faithful Families*. Also visit www.traci-smith.com/resources for a complete list of other Bibles, books, websites, and other resources that might be used to provide families with tools they can use to support faith development at home. Consider providing a handout with those resources or talking specifically about resources your faith community has access to.

# Notes

**Bedtime: Night Time Blessing**
[1]Adapted from Numbers 6:24–26.
[2]Adapted from Philippians 4:6.
[3]Inspired by Romans 15:13.

**Moving Out/Going to College: Taking the Essentials**
[4]Hebrews 11:1.

**Family Ceremony to Mark a Divorce**
[5]Adapted from Jeremiah 29:11 (NIV).

**The Daily Office: Morning and Evening Prayer**
[6]Some pronouns changed to be gender inclusive.

**Imagination: Star Pictures**
[7]Hebrews 11:1, NRSV.
[8]Psalm 147:4, (NIV).
[9]Genesis 9:14–15a, (NIV).

## Our Family's Special Traditions

*Use these pages to record the special faith moments that are unique to your family. Those might be holiday traditions of your family, recipes handed down for generations, prayers in the family Bible, ideas for traditions you'd like to start, etc.*

 *Our Family's Special Traditions*

*Our Family's Special Traditions*

*Our Family's Special Traditions*

*Our Family's Special Traditions*

*Our Family's Special Traditions*

"In a culture that has become isolating, technological, fractious, and cold Traci Smith has given us a survival kit of practices to help families stay close to what is sacred, meaningful, intimate, and alive. *Faithful Families* will not only help parents nurture the souls of their children, it will keep them sane within the chaotic forces of 21st century family life."
—Mark Yaconelli, author of *The Gift of Hard Things* and *Contemplative Youth Ministry*

"This book is a must-have for any family wishing to live as faithful disciples of Jesus. Traci Smith has created a gold mine of resources, ideas, and practices that invite children, teens, parents, grandparents, aunts, uncles, cousins, houseguests, pets—everyone who makes up all kinds of families—to actively form one another in authentic Christian faith. Get this book for your family. Give it to families in your faith community. Drop copies of it from an airplane. It's sure to have an impact on all who use it."
—David M. Csinos, assistant professor of practical theology at Atlantic School of Theology and founder of Faith Forward

"We all want to teach our children about gratitude, hospitality, and generosity. We want them to have a sense of wonder and to see how they are connected to something beyond themselves. Yet it is hard to know how to counter society's emphasis on consumerism, wealth, and fame. Traci Smith teaches us how to slow down, to create sacred space and time in order to nurture a child's soul. *Faithful Families* is a gift of the spirit."

— Rabbi Sandy Eisenberg Sasso, author of *God's Paintbrush, Creation's First Light,* and many other award-winning children's books

"*Faithful Families* makes me wish I had a time machine so I could go back eleven years and start all of these practices as a brand-new parent. Thankfully this book covers countless ways to bring spiritual vitality to your family's life right now, exactly where you are, whether that's dealing with diapers, driving, or anything in between. Traci is a gracious guide through practices that are simple, profound, and welcoming."
— MaryAnn McKibben Dana, author of *Sabbath in the Suburbs: A Family's Experiment with Holy Time*

"*Faithful Families* is full of helpful ideas for how to support the faith growth of your children through home traditions and ceremonies. These suggestions are offered with the theological sensitivity of a pastor and with the practical eye of a parent who knows what will and won't work with a busy family. Any family serious about making faith a more visible part of their family life will be able to find things here that will work for them."

— Robert J. Keeley, Calvin College, and author of *Helping Our Children Grow in Faith*

The Young Clergy Women International (YCWI) Series features writings from young adult clergy women on topics that give meaning to their lives and ministries. YCWI includes women from around the world who are committed to serving God and supporting one another. Visit YCWI online at youngclergywomen.org.

## Other Books from the YCWI Series

### Blessed Are the Crazy
Breaking the Silence about Mental Illness, Family, and Church
*by Sarah Griffith Lund*

### Any Day a Beautiful Change
A Story of Faith and Family
*by Katherine Willis Pershey*

### Bless Her Heart
Life As a Young Clergy Woman
*by Ashley-Anne Masters and Stacy Smith*

### Making Paper Cranes
Toward an Asian American Feminist Theology
*by Mihee Kim-Kort*

### Sabbath in the Suburbs
A Family's Experiment with Holy Time
*by MaryAnn McKibben Dana*

### Who's Got Time?
Spirituality for a Busy Generation
*by Teri Peterson and Amy Fetterman*